Nigger Heaven

Nigger Heaven

BY

CARL VAN VECHTEN

Introduction by Kathleen Pfeiffer

UNIVERSITY OF ILLINOIS PRESS
Urbana and Chicago

First Illinois paperback edition, 2000

Manufactured in the United States of America
∞ This book is printed on acid-free paper.

Library of Congress Cataloging-in-Publication Data
Van Vechten, Carl, 1880–1964.
Nigger heaven / by Carl Van Vechten ; introduction by
Kathleen Pfeiffer.
p. cm.
ISBN 0-252-06860-2 (pbk. : alk. paper)
ISBN 978-0-252-06860-7 (pbk. : alk. paper)
1. Afro-Americans—New York (State)—New York Fiction. 2. Harlem
(New York, N.Y.)—Fiction. I. Title.
PS3543.A653N5 2000
813'.52—dc21 99-36777
CIP
P 8 7 6 5 4

For Fania Marinoff

"All day long and all night through
One thing only must I do:
Quench my pride and cool my blood,
Lest I perish in the flood."

—Countee Cullen

Introduction

KATHLEEN PFEIFFER

Nigger Heaven reaffirms the importance of not judging a book by its cover. That many readers did so explains the tumult it caused some seventy years ago, and there is good reason to believe that many readers will judge it harshly again today. That will be a shame, because Carl Van Vechten's popular book accomplished a great deal of good precisely because of its controversial title. At heart a sincere and earnest appeal on behalf of black America's enormous talent and simultaneous frustration, *Nigger Heaven* is cloaked ironically in epithet and cliché. But we ought not confuse the book's intentions with the evocations in its title. Effectively disguised as tawdry sensationalism, the best-selling novel drew unsuspecting white readers in droves; after feeding white America's expectations with some two dozen pages following a free-strutting pimp on the prowl, it shifts decisively into a world of middle-class respectability, where Harlem is defined by intellectual values and professional ambition. The black actress Edna Thomas understood this well, and wrote to Van Vechten, "Fool the public if you must darling; but you and I know that you've gotten a lot of propaganda off your chest, don't we?"[1] Alain Locke concurred, writing, "It's art—but at the same time sub-cutaneous propaganda."[2] Thomas and Locke understood Van Vechten's accomplishment clearly: a craftily packaged progressive discourse that sought greater understanding between the races.

Van Vechten's notebooks indicate that *Nigger Heaven* was not the only title he considered: during his research and note-gathering, he evaluated a number of possibilities, including "The Great Black Walled City," "White Tar," and "Rest Yo Coat." But alongside these other possible titles, he cites a passage from *Folk Beliefs of the Southern Negro* which states, "Nigger Heaven is an American slang expression for the topmost gallery of a theatre, so called because in certain of the United States, Negroes are arbitrarily forced to sit in these cheap seats. . . . The geographical position of Harlem, the Negro quarter of New York, corresponds to the location of the gallery in a theatre." Van Vechten underlines the words "are arbitrarily forced" and notes beside them, "The title of the novel derives from this fact."[3] Alfred A. Knopf accommodated the author's request for advance publicity which emphasized this gallery metaphor. One representative Knopf *Borzoi Broadside* promotes the novel as a "fascinating and inscrutable drama that takes place in the gallery of the vast theatre of New York—from which the white world below can be seen, but which it cannot see."[4] Illustrator Aaron Douglas underscored the theater imagery in the drawings he prepared for *Nigger Heaven*'s advertisement in white periodicals (fig. 1). But in a significant contrast, Knopf used a different Douglas print to advertise the novel in journals read primarily by blacks; this other illustration emphasized the novel's universal appeal over its specific location. Charles Scruggs argues that this image, "Harlem as a potential Heavenly City ('nigger *heaven*')," underscores its mythical themes (fig. 2).[5]

Opposite: Figure 1. Image by Aaron Douglas which appeared in periodicals appealing to mostly white audiences. In the James Weldon Johnson Collection, Yale Collection of American Literature, Beinecke Rare Book and Manuscript Library, Yale University. Reproduced courtesy of the library.

NIGGER HEAVEN
BY CARL VAN VECHTEN

NIGGER HEAVEN

BY CARL VAN VECHTEN

Clearly, the advertising appeals to readers of both races proved effective. Initially banned in Boston, *Nigger Heaven* achieved an immediate sellout of sixteen thousand copies, and its success necessitated nine printings in the first four months after it appeared. The novel became a locus for angry protests, and numerous debates followed in its wake—not all of them hinged on its literary value. W. E. B. Du Bois's review of the novel—an influential and oft-cited response—argues that the book does violence to black folk. "Carl Van Vechten's 'Nigger Heaven' is a blow in the face," he charges.[6] And indeed, anecdotes of its reception and influence bear this out. Just one month after that review appeared, for instance, Professor S. R. Williams of Wilberforce College brought a copy of the novel to a Harlem rally which protested a particularly brutal triple lynching in the South. As the *New York Times* reported on December 20, 1926, the inflammatory novel received similarly inflammatory treatment:

> After reading several passages Williams asked what should be done with them to show proper resentment of their contents.
>
> When a chorus of voices shouted "Burn 'em up!" he ignited the two pieces of paper and held them aloft until the flames consumed them. He said that the two pages were perhaps the most objectionable in the book but that there might be a later ceremony for the burning of the entire book.

The apparently illogical association—*Nigger Heaven* never addresses lynching—nevertheless reflects the deeply felt emotional logic through which the novel functioned as a site to contest racial violence.

Opposite: Figure 2. Image by Aaron Douglas which appeared in periodicals appealing to mostly black audiences. In the James Weldon Johnson Collection, Yale Collection of American Literature, Beinecke Rare Book and Manuscript Library, Yale University. Reproduced courtesy of the library.

Concern about the title dominated the author's thoughts as he composed. Carl Van Vechten knew what he was getting himself into when he chose his title, and he recognized the deeply offensive implications of the word "nigger." Whether the term is used aggressively to express racial hatred or ironically to destabilize racial hatred, to use "nigger" is to evoke a history of brutality, oppression, and dehumanization; as long as that history exists, "nigger" can never be a mere word. The reactions of Van Vechten's many black friends underscored the truth of this. As early as November 25, 1925—before the first draft was even completed—he notes in his daybooks that he "[t]old a few people about the title" at a party the night before. That night, he writes, "I spring my title on Grace Johnson, etc. She says it will be hated." Likewise, on November 27, his friend Countee Cullen, whose poetry provides the novel's epigraph, "turned white with rage." Though Van Vechten tried to explain his perspective, Cullen's distress eventually led to a break in their friendship. Rosamond Johnson suggested the alternative "Black Man's Heab'n," but Van Vechten rejected the idea, jotting in his notes that it "unfortunately omits to suggest the ironic symbolism of the title actually used." By contrast, Walter White admired the title and wished he'd thought of it first.

Van Vechten was, then, well aware of the risk he ran to offend. His own father, understanding his son's ironic intentions, had pleaded with him in two emotional letters to remove the epithet. "Your 'Nigger Heaven' is a title I don't like," Charles Duane Van Vechten wrote in late November, 1925, as the book was in its final draft. "I have myself never spoken of a colored man as a 'nigger.' If you are trying to help the race, as I am assured you are, I think every word you write should be a respectful one towards the blacks." One week later, he wrote again, in the feeble script of an ill man, to reiterate his point:

> Please bear in mind what I am about to have the courage to say to you. It is the *last* word I shall ever say to you on the subject—I note what you have to say about the title to your new book, including that statement that some of your negro friends agree with me—You are accustomed to "get away" with what you undertake to do: but you do not *always* succeed; and my belief is that this will be another failure, *if* you persist in your *"I shall use it nevertheless[.]"* Whatever you may be compelled to say *in* the book, your present title will not be understood & I feel certain you should change it.[7]

In spite of the pained reactions of his friends and father, Van Vechten remained committed to his title's ironic value. Even late in his life he insisted, "It was used ironically, of course, and irony is not something that most Negroes understand, especially the ones who write for the papers."[8] In Van Vechten's mind, the apparently racist allusions suggested in its provocative title must be understood in context; and indeed, *Nigger Heaven* actually spends only thirty-nine of its 284 pages depicting raunchy or debauched aspects of Harlem life.

While Van Vechten may have underestimated the pain his title might inflict, he was well aware of its nuances. It has often been noted that Van Vechten encouraged Ronald Firbank to retitle his 1924 novel *Sorrow in Sunlight* with the inflammatory title *Prancing Nigger* in order to increase its market appeal, but it is just as important to note that neither *Prancing Nigger* nor Clement Woods's 1922 *Nigger* (nor, for that matter, Joseph Conrad's 1897 *Nigger of the Narcissus*) received the volume or intensity of criticism which followed Van Vechten's novel, then or now. The facts of his life and the legacy of his work make it impossible for us to dismiss him as racist; indeed, Van Vechten seems to have sympathized deeply—however shortsightedly—with racial suffering. In one poignant instance, Van Vechten records in his daybooks a nightmare which haunted him on September 24, 1926, two weeks after the novel's appearance. "We talked about Nigger Heaven all evening," he writes. "I go to bed about one and dream I am a nigger, being chased in race riots." None of Van Vechten's private writings offer any hint of racial hatred or prejudice or bias. To the contrary, he was a tireless promoter of integration, an enthusiastic patron of black art and artists, and a dedicated collector of African American memorabilia. Van Vechten's biographer, Bruce Kellner, notes that in the process of revising his manuscript, "Passages were cut that might adversely reflect on the Negro in the eyes of white readers; for example, 'We're most of us lazy, and indirect, and careless, and if we get anywhere it's usually luck.'"[9]

Nigger Heaven was not the only Harlem Renaissance novel to elicit strong reactions from race-conscious readers. Claude McKay's 1928 *Home to Harlem* received a similarly vituperative review from Du Bois, who charged in *The Crisis* that McKay's book left him feeling "distinctly like taking a bath."[10] McKay's black Jamaican ancestry and his novel's uncontroversial title make it difficult for us to dismiss the issues raised by Du Bois in relation to Van Vechten and *Nigger Heaven* as merely topical. Rather, Du Bois's response to both novels was firmly grounded in his philosophy of race, a political aesthetic which held that "all art is propaganda and ever must be."[11] For Du Bois, any art which focused on the black experience carried with it political implications and would, therefore, necessarily either promote or inhibit the race. The "bounden duty" of black artists—or of any artist who endeavored to depict or comment on black culture—was, Du Bois argued, "to begin this great work of the creation of beauty, of the preservation of beauty, of the realization of beauty."[12] And Du Bois's Victorian sensibility found little beauty in either *Nigger Heaven* or *Home to Harlem*. Many black readers also charged McKay with crimes similar to Van Vechten's—obscenity, crass commercial exploitation, betrayal of his race. Thus it would be both imprudent and inaccurate to dismiss the controversy over *Nigger Heaven* as a response to either Van Vechten's title or his racial identity, for it is clear that more resonant tensions were also at work.

Still, many of *Nigger Heaven*'s early readers responded most emphatically to the troubling title. Many of Van Vechten's friends, both black and white, agreed with his father that the title should be changed. James Weldon Johnson's comments on the manuscript prior to publication suggest that within the novel itself, "Use of 'nigger' as forbidden to whites might be shown."[13] "I hope you won't put me out of your favor, when I confess I was nervous about this book," one woman wrote. "It sounded dangerous!"[14] Charles Johnson noted, "I might make a stir about your title and be a good 'race man' but fundamentally I am too anxious to have the sting of the term extracted in the fashion that such employment promises to do it."[15] The *Pittsburgh Courier* initially refused to advertise it, until Walter White intervened. Fifteen years after the novel appeared, Langston Hughes continued to grapple with the deeply painful connotations implicit in the title. "The word *nigger* to colored people of high and low degree is like a red rag to a bull," he notes in his autobiography. "Used rightly or wrongly, ironically or seriously, of necessity for the sake of realism, or impishly for the sake of comedy, it doesn't matter. Negroes do not like it in any book or play whatsoever, be the book or play ever so sympathetic in its treatment of the basic problems of the race."[16] James Weldon Johnson agrees in his autobiography, explaining, "Most of the Negroes who condemned *Nigger Heaven* did not read it; they were estopped by the title. I don't think they would now be so sensitive about it; as the race progresses it will become less and less susceptible to hurts from such causes."[17] Johnson was wise and insightful on many counts, but the history of race relations in the United States in the late twentieth century definitively contradicts his prediction. "Nigger" continues to be a highly charged, divisive, multivalent term, and *Nigger Heaven* offers us, among other things, an opportunity to revisit and locate our discussions about its import.

The self-aggrandizement of *Nigger Heaven*'s title is entirely in keeping with Van Vechten's flamboyant life; so, too, is the novel's implicit racial progressivism. His was a reformative family, his mother having been a friend of the abolitionist and feminist Lucy Stone; his father was a conscientious man whose liberal racial attitude led him to finance the Piney Woods School in Mississippi as well as to insist that the family address their black laundress as "Mrs. Sercy" and the gardener as "Mr. Oliphant," rather than calling them by more familiar names, as was the demeaning custom. Carl took his father's lessons in equality and racial integration to heart while at the University of Chicago, where he met the black singer and dancer Carrie Washington (who later assumed the stage name Carita Day) and her husband Ernest Hogan, a performer who incensed black audiences with his popular song "All Coons Look Alike to Me." Van Vechten would bring the pair to fraternity dances. "He would play the piano for her singing and she would dance with everybody," Van Vechten later commented. "Nobody had any objections to dancing with Negroes at that epoch. It's probably because I never asked them whether or not they did object."[18]

Carl Van Vechten thus demonstrated interest in black culture long before he ever conceived of *Nigger Heaven*. His early writing career as an assistant music critic and a dance critic for the *New York Times* brought him to numerous performances and allowed him to hone the critical skills that would later inform his sense of a black aesthetic. Van Vechten valued artistic innovation highly and found much to praise in emerging black theatrical productions. Relatively few black performances were running during his early years as a critic, but as they became popular, Van Vechten celebrated their distinctly Negro characteristics. His theater criticism, for instance, advocates the use of vernacular on stage and of a dark or multihued chorus. Van Vechten's boundless enthusiasm gave public voice to the swelling of attention in the 1920s to productions like the Darktown Follies and Shuffle Along. Similarly, his laudatory and didactic review of James Weldon Johnson's *Book of American Negro Spirituals* insists that dialect "is an integral part of the charm of these naive songs."[19] He published two prescient pieces about the blues in 1925, not only to educate his white readership but also to promote the musical innovations he so valued.

Throughout his life, Carl Van Vechten maintained the uncanny knack of being at the right place at the right time, often for the first time: he befriended Mabel Dodge one month before her Sixty Ninth Regiment Armory Show; he met Gertrude Stein and Alice B. Toklas in Paris after the three shared a box at the second performance of the notorious *Sacre du Printemps;*[20] he aligned himself with Alfred A. Knopf in 1916, as the young publisher was launching his fledgling press. And Carl Van Vechten's long-standing interest in black America pointed him toward Harlem just as the excitement was beginning. H. L. Mencken accompanied Van Vechten on one of his first trips into Harlem, in early 1924, where the two drank all night at speakeasies. In the late summer of 1924, Knopf arranged for Van Vechten to meet, at the latter's explicit request, Walter A. White, after Van Vechten read and admired White's *The Fire in the Flint.* Van Vechten and White became fast friends, and while the friendship was genuine (White named his son Carl Darrow after both Van Vechten and Clarence Darrow) it also served both men quite well, giving Van Vechten access to the Harlem in which he was, by then, so "violently interested," and giving White access to Van Vechten's own influential white friends. "There is always something in New York," he wrote Gertrude Stein in Paris, "and this winter it is Negro poets and jazz pianists."[21] Walter White took Van Vechten to an important cabaret party, an NAACP event at Happy Rhone's in November of 1924, where Carlo, as the writer was known to his friends, met James Weldon Johnson, Langston Hughes, and many other important Harlem personalities; he quickly became a fixture of Harlem's nightlife.

"But it soon became obvious to me," Van Vechten later recalled, "that I would write about these people because my feeling about them was very strong."[22] Van Vechten and his wife, the Russian-born actress Fania Marinoff, hosted numerous integrated parties at their home, and they became regulars at Small's Paradise, a cabaret at 2294 Seventh Avenue which featured nightly jam sessions, double entendre blues singers, and waiters who delivered trays of drinks while dancing the Charleston. As Van Vechten participated in Harlem's culture, he became part of its folklore. Lyrics in the popular Andy Razaf song "Go Harlem" documented his interest, encouraging listeners to "go inspectin' like Van Vechten." A favored anecdote of the time features a conversation between a black porter and a white woman. "Good morning, Mrs. Astor," he says, picking up her luggage. "How do you know my name, young man?" she asks. "Why, ma'am, I met you last week at Carl Van Vechten's." As was his style when integrating parties at college, Van Vechten rarely asked his guests whether they approved of such mixing, he simply did it. "I just invite them," he declared, "I do not apologize for my friends."[23]

Once he joined Harlem's community of artists, writers, musicians, and intellectuals, Van Vechten redoubled his efforts to cultivate a white audience for black art. *Vanity Fair* published his essay "Moanin' Wid a Sword in Mah Han'" in February of 1926, as part of this effort. "Moanin'" emphasizes the points Van Vechten made in earlier analyses of black art, not only explaining the richness and complexity of black art forms but also warning against their potential exploitation by the cultural poaching of white America. "It is significant," he notes, "that the great Negroes almost invariably climb to fame with material which is the heritage of their race."[24] Van Vechten's review of Alain Locke's important anthology *The New Negro* underscores this point, warning that "if the Negro writers don't utilize the wealth of material at their fingertips, white writers, naturally, will be only too eager to exploit it." But while this review extols the Negro's unique contributions, it also reveals Van Vechten's contradictory presumption that the races are essentially similar. "Negroes among themselves," he muses, "behave and react very much as white people, *of the same class*, behave and react among themselves."[25]

Such liberal attitudes toward race defied the segregationist logic of the time. Following law and social custom, most Americans drew sharp distinctions between black and white, but Van Vechten maintained a color-blind disposition, noting, "I never thought of things, that way, you know; I never think of people as Negroes. I think of them as friends."[26] In developing *Nigger Heaven*'s characters, he likewise drew connections between black and white when everyone else in his Jim Crow culture was drawing distinctions. In its earliest stages, Van Vechten's plan for the novel modeled fictional black characters by synthesizing blacks and whites of his acquaintance. "The most fascinating and amusing of all Negroes is Nora Ray who reminds me so much of Mary Garden," he wrote Fania, referring to the white opera singer whose musical interpretations he greatly admired.[27] As he developed the novel's black characters, Van Vechten noted, "it never occurred to me that they would behave differently than other people. I wrote about them exactly as if they were white."[28] While this statement seems profoundly caucacentric according to our contemporary racial consciousness, it was, in its time, a mark of dramatic racial progressivism.

However, no matter how truly well intentioned Van Vechten's racial attitudes may have been—and they were wholly sincere and distinctly progressive—they both contradicted and undermined those members of the "New Negro" movement who sought to create and validate a distinctly black identity. Locke's *New Negro,* published one year before *Nigger Heaven,* sought to shape a black aesthetic. Both explicitly and by example, each of the volume's contributors support Locke's central assertion in "The Negro Takes His Place in American Art" that no "art idiom, however universal, grows in a cultural vacuum; each, however great, always has some rootage and flavor of a particular soil and personality. And just as it has been a critical necessity to foster the development of a national character in the American art of our time, by the very same logic and often by the very same means, it has been reasonable and necessary to promote and quicken the racial motive and inspiration of the hitherto isolated and disparaged Negro artist."[29]

Race-conscious blacks embraced a number of strategies for social progress, ranging from Locke's cultural pluralism to Du Bois's focus on beautiful art. To such an audience, then, for Carl Van Vechten to imagine black characters as fundamentally the same as white ones was for him to ignore the brutal realities of a world which constantly reminded them of their difference. Mark Helbling has argued that the conflicted reactions to *Nigger Heaven* emerge from precisely this tension—from the contest between Van Vechten's depiction of a distinctly black idiom (the sort he advocated in his musical criticism and in the pages of *Vanity Fair*) and his countermanding belief that all characters, regardless of color, should be imagined and treated as if they are white.[30]

From the start, Van Vechten conceived of *Nigger Heaven* as a mediation between black and white America, innovative in its frank representation of Harlem's heretofore invisible black community. He explained his conception in some detail to Gertrude Stein, writing "This will not be a novel about Negroes in the South or white contacts or lynchings. It will be about NEGROES, as they live now in the new city of Harlem (which is part of New York). About 400,000 of them live here now, rich and poor, fast and slow, intellectual and ignorant."[31] Van Vechten's letters to other friends document his insecurity about the project and indicate his awareness of his own cultural and experiential limitations. Around May of 1925, he wrote to Langston Hughes about the project, noting that he felt "rather alarmed." "It would have been comparatively easy for me to write it before I knew as much as I know now," he observed, "enough to know that I am thoroughly ignorant!"[32] He reiterated this insecurity in a letter to Fania Marinoff: "If I write my Negro novel, and sometimes the difficulties frighten me, I am going to dedicate it to you."[33] By early September of 1925, he still hadn't begun writing, and noted wryly to Hughes, "Something seems to hold me back."[34]

But once he started writing, he composed in a great fervor. On November 3, 1925, almost a year to the day after he met Harlem's greatest dignitaries, Van Vechten commenced and noted the inauguration in his daybooks: "I begin work on Nigger Heaven and write most of the first chapter before lunch." In a week of nonstop writing, he drafted the first four chapters and prologue. He completed a draft and two revisions of *Nigger Heaven* in three months, and reviewed its page proofs in three separate readings. He worked steadily and fast, composing daily, all the while reading a range of literature which would inform the novel's concerns: the African American folk tales in Charles Chesnutt's *The Conjure Woman;* the realistic treatment of ambition in Theodore Dreiser's *An American Tragedy;* the satirical critique of social convention in Jonathan Swift's *Gulliver's Travels;* the complex analysis of racial identity in James Weldon Johnson's *The Autobiography of an Ex-Colored Man.*

Van Vechten's own experiences in Harlem and his black friends provided the insights ("family secrets" as Charles Johnson would call them) into the private experiences of black America which gave his novel the ring of racial "authenticity." His drunken nights at speakeasies constituted research, and he regularly listened to blues records "for phrases and instrumental effects" to use in the novel. Both the notebooks in which he recorded his plans for the novel and the daybooks in which he recorded his daily activities acknowledge the influence of W. E. B. Du Bois's and Charles Chesnutt's fiction. Yet Van Vechten's notebooks also anticipate the possibility that *Nigger Heaven* might be received as a politically charged work. "This is not a propaganda novel," he notes. "It is neither pro-Negro or pro-anything else. It purports to show what might happen to two young people under certain circumstances. Incidentally it presents such a picture of Harlem, the great black walled city, as has not yet been painted."[35]

The writer and physician Rudolph Fisher and James Weldon Johnson both read and commented on the manuscript, offering suggestions for revision prior to its publication. One of James Weldon Johnson's striking suggestions which Van Vechten adopted encourages revisions which make the final scene more brutal and graphically violent. "How would it do to show Byron as Pettijohn enters Black Venus and draws near," he writes, "and unable to draw his revolver—but when he sees Pettijohn shot and bleeding on the floor, he is seized by another emotion and stomps the dying man in the face and empties his revolver into him?"[36] Fisher told Van Vechten that the novel's beginning was "too pro-Negro" and suggested several bits of "Harlemese," like the Negro understanding that "pink" is "also used to mean a colored girl that can pass for white."[37]

Van Vechten's difficulty in grappling with *Nigger Heaven*'s inherent complexities was surely exacerbated by the considerable distress which then affected his personal life. Shortly after he completed the novel's first draft, his father died rather suddenly, just following their exchange over the title; early that spring, his much-loved cat died, too (Van Vechten's seventh book had been a tribute to cats). Soon afterwards, his volatile relationship with his wife Fania Marinoff reached a painful nadir during which she left him; it was an agonizing two days before she returned. "She says she is through for ever," he wrote in his daybook on June 24. "If she is what is there in life for me?" Van Vechten fretted about *Nigger Heaven* all the while, and his letters to Langston Hughes articulate these concerns. "I'm very unsettled about Nigger Heaven," he wrote Hughes. "I get too emotional when writing it and what one needs in writing is a calm, cold eye."[38] Even once the manuscript was completed, Van Vechten's troubles continued. While his friend and publisher Alfred Knopf was generally receptive to Van Vechten's work, he was less than enthusiastic about *Nigger Heaven* once he read it through; after Knopf agreed to publish the book, the manuscript was checked by lawyers so that its questionable or purportedly obscene passages could be cut or revised.

This edition of the novel is its seventh printing, a significantly different—and for many scholars, far more valuable—version than the first. Because Van Vechten neglected to obtain proper permission to reprint lyrics from the popular song "Shake That Thing," the novel's first five printings contained those lyrics at the expense of copyright liability. Considering the overwhelming popularity of the immediate bestseller, author and publisher both sought an amiable settlement with Shapiro Bernstein, the firm suing for copyright infringement. Van Vechten coped with the crisis by visiting Knopf's offices daily, drinking often, and, eventually, by telephoning his friend Langston Hughes, who was then studying at Lincoln University, for help in replacing the questionable passages. Hughes obliged Van Vechten (to whom he was indebted, since Van Vechten encouraged and facilitated the poet's own publication) by traveling to Van Vechten's apartment, where the two passed an intense twenty-four hours as Hughes composed verse to fit the novel as needed, line for line. Hughes's verse replaced the lyrics of "Shake That Thing" and of one or two other songs in the novel's sixth printing. The seventh edition contains these plus the remainder of Hughes's replacement lyrics, the early work of a poet who went on to become one of the century's best; Van Vechten's note following the glossary indicates which pages include Hughes's contributions.[39]

Van Vechten's desire to reach both black and white readers can be seen in the implicit argument of the novel's structure: while the prologue opens in the street with the pimpish Scarlet Creeper and passes briefly through a sleazy cabaret and a rowdy party, these are the peripheral scenes and they move quickly. The heart of the novel, and the ideological center of black Harlem, emerges in the stories of Mary Love and Byron Kasson, each of whom struggles with the injustice of racial segregation, and both of whom, like Van Vechten, are themselves newcomers to Harlem. Mary, a cultured, intellectual, and race-conscious librarian, maintains the sort of conservative, Victorian sensibility which racially progressive black readers appreciated; yet Mary defies easy categorization, as she simultaneously lauds the African and African American art, writing, and music that drew white America's attention to Harlem. Van Vechten limns Byron Kasson's racial conflict more explicitly in terms of literary ambition. A frustrated aspiring writer, Byron struggles unsuccessfully to overcome deep ambivalence about his racial identity and seeks—unsuccessfully—racially neutral material for his fiction. A range of settings illustrate Harlem's richness and variety: we see Mary and Byron in the library, at home having thoughtful conversations with young professionals, fulfilling social obligations, courting in Central Park. The novel is peopled with a range of characters wide and varied enough to appeal to a broad, biracial audience.

Nigger Heaven jabs at its own fictional boundaries by situating its characters in a real and familiar neighborhood, so that individual characters identifiably caricature Harlem's most famous (and more often, infamous) personages. James Weldon Johnson once plotted out a list which proved to be, as Bruce Kellner has noted, deadly accurate. Johnson identified Van Vechten's intended resemblances between many characters; contemporary readers may be most drawn to the novel's Adora Boniface, a stand-in for A'Leila Walker, the Harlem heiress whose mother, Madame C. J. Walker, invented the famous hair-straightening process; in Russett Durwood, one sees H. L. Mencken; and in Lasca Sartoris, one sees a portrait of a former cabaret singer, the notoriously oft-married, scandalous Nora Holt.[40] Holt's own letter to Van Vechten from Paris underscores the connection. "The cries of protest from the Harlemites reach me even in Paris," she writes. "I am also subjected to the exasperation of friends—My God Nora you have broken out again—this time in Carl Van Vechten's new novel—What will you do next?"[41]

The Harlem in *Nigger Heaven* also merges with other fictional worlds of black and white: Mimi Daquin, who is the heroine of Walter White's contemporaneous novel *Flight*, appears at one of *Nigger Heaven*'s parties; Gareth Johns, the fictional version of Van

Vechten himself who was the leading male character in Van Vechten's *The Tattooed Countess,* makes a cameo appearance here, as he does in *Parties* and *Firecrackers.* Van Vechten's text thus evokes a number of writers, artists, and musicians who themselves experimented with form and challenged conventional notions of aesthetic structure. Van Vechten was known to declare that cataloguing was an important part of his personality, and this predisposition shapes *Nigger Heaven* with its pastiche of black and white: the poetry of Wallace Stevens, the art of Picasso, and the music of Stravinsky are drawn into the same narrative whole as musician Rosamond Johnson and singer Taylor Gordon. These references map out a literary intersection of race and culture, demonstrating the ease with which Gertrude Stein and Charles Chesnutt can complement each other's work, thereby demonstrating too the richness of a racially hybrid literary culture. This is as true in references to literature and art as to the popular musical and theatrical performers of the day.

Nigger Heaven is thus a distinctly self-conscious novel, and its numerous extratextual devices appeal to readers of both races by either complicating or undermining their apparent assertions. Van Vechten provides ostensibly scholarly footnotes which claim to interpret black culture for the white reader; the very first footnote points readers to "a glossary of the unusual Negro words and phrases employed in this novel." What the glossary accomplishes, however, is more in keeping with the African American trickster tradition than any scholarly endeavor. This is best illustrated in the twinned entries "*boody:* see hootchie-pap" and "*hootchie-pap:* see boody." The promised rhetorical explanations are inside jokes which prove more enigmatic than intelligible. The glossary points in sum to the larger project of the novel itself—to offer a glimpse into the contours of black culture, but to obscure and thereby protect the integrity of that culture's meaning. Such winks to readers—black and white both—infuse *Nigger Heaven* with energy and contradiction, and the effect was dramatic, not only for black readers who wondered how a white man had access to such insights. Two women from Mount Holyoke wrote Van Vechten to ask about the true meaning of "boody" and "hootchie-pap," colloquial references to sex. By contrast, the singer and writer Taylor Gordon laughs about Van Vechten's familiarity with color designations. "And on page 208," he writes, "I liked to croaked when you begin to use, spade lingo, spagingy, spagade, and when did a pious young man like you learn the interpretation of, Hootchie-pap, surely you never was a merchant were you? Ha Ha, and bought a little brown goods, or maybe some Black Velvet."[42]

To be sure, Van Vechten's narrative presumptuously participates in a distinctly African American literary tradition in which coded language allows the black underclass to maintain a separate and thereby self-empowering counter discourse. In one of the earliest African American–authored novels, *Iola Leroy,* Frances Harper presents the idea as "market speech," a code devised by slaves to communicate information about the Civil War's progress surreptitiously. *Nigger Heaven*'s black readers may have reacted so strongly to what Nora Holt identified as the novel's uncanny insights because Van Vechten was giving away information to which he wasn't culturally entitled. But the variety of conflicted responses registered by *Nigger Heaven*'s readers not only reflect its inherent esotericism, they also—and perhaps more importantly—indicate that Van Vechten tapped into some deep and powerful cultural emotions. Mild responses were rare, and many readers were repulsed and offended by those very elements which appealed to others.

Yet Van Vechten found some support—and *Nigger Heaven* received praise—from within Harlem, as is evidenced by numerous correspondences. The Urban League founder and sociologist Charles Johnson wrote to Van Vechten, noting, "I don't seem to find much to object to in *Nigger Heaven,* and I am almost ashamed of the excess of enthusiasm to which I was tempted."[43] Charles Chesnutt wrote a particularly complimentary letter, noting, "As to the literary quality of the work, it is done with your usual vividness and sparkle." Chesnutt concluded by "hoping it may have the success which its brilliancy and obvious honesty deserve."[44] The writer Eric Walrond sent a telegram: "I HAVE JUST READ NIGGER HEAVEN AND I CANNOT DENY THE IMPULSE TO TELL YOU HOW MUCH I ENJOYED IT THE HARLEM IT DESCRIBES IS ACCURATELY CREDITABLY GLAMOROUSLY ENSHRINED."[45] Paul Robeson also sent a telegram, effusive: "DEAR CARLO NIGGER HEAVEN AMAZING IN ITS ABSOLUTE UNDERSTANDING AND DEEP SYMPATHY THANKS FOR SUCH A BOOK ANXIOUS TO TALK ABOUT IT."[46] James Weldon Johnson offered his friend his unflagging public support, arguing in an *Opportunity* review that "the author pays colored people the rare tribute of writing about them as people rather than as puppets." Johnson insisted that "the book and not the title is the thing," explaining "If the book has a thesis, it is: Negroes are people; they have the same passions, the same shortcomings, the same aspirations, the same gradations of social strata as other people."[47]

Indeed, Van Vechten's own racial identity was, in many cases, the single most salient factor in determining its reception. The philanthropist lawyer Arthur Spingarn, an active participant in the NAACP, wrote that there was "no book in English (by ofay or jig) about Negro life that could compare with it, whether for knowledge of its milieu or for fine objective sympathy."[48] Many readers were preoccupied with the question of whether "ofay" (a colloquial reference to white people which derives from pig Latin for "foe") or "jig" could have written the novel. Walter White's congratulatory telegram addresses its praise "AS ONE RACE AUTHOR TO ANOTHER."[49] Charles Johnson's comment that he "wish[ed] a Negro had written it" was echoed in Nella Larsen Imes's more dramatic lament, "Why, oh, why, couldn't we have done something as big as this for ourselves?"[50] But where Van Vechten's black friends pondered the political implications of its author's race, his white friends expressed great amusement over his apparent joke. The playwright Avery Hopwood wrote, "Of course, everyone is bound to ask how you acquired such an intimate knowledge of Harlem, and to say, 'Why, he must have lived there!' I am explaining to them, however, that that is not the case—that you really see little of Harlem, these days, but that you saw a great deal of it before you *passed*. They are all so surprised to hear about your negro strain, but I tell them that your best friends *always knew*. . . . And no matter how other people treat you, I shall remain the same."[51]

Hopwood's joking intimation that Van Vechten was actually black and passing for white was a more shrewd insight than he knew, since the author did identify with Dick Sill, *Nigger Heaven*'s passing character. Van Vechten's own argument about the white press's interest in black writers, articulated in the *Vanity Fair* essay titled "Moanin' Wid a Sword in Mah Han'," mirrors Dick Sill's comments about the issue almost exactly. Little wonder, since Van Vechten wrote the *Vanity Fair* essay just two weeks after he drafted the chapter where Dick explains his views.

An illustrated issue of the novel was planned in 1930 and E. McKnight Kauffer prepared a series of prints which are now part of the permanent collection at the Museum of Modern Art in New York. That lavish edition never appeared, however, because when the depression hit, such a publishing venture became risky.

The novel was translated into nearly a dozen languages; in 1951, it appeared as an inexpensive Avon paperback edition. The cover blurbs on that small volume emphasize precisely those aspects of the novel which brought it such inaccurate publicity some twenty-five years earlier; Avon's presentation is downright histrionic, with the front cover declaring it a "strange, arresting, and tremendously shockingly serious story," and the back cover asking ominously, "What is Responsible for the Unleashed Passions of Old Harlem?" While the cover illustration was benign enough, its breathless, gushing rhetoric extols the novel's cultural authority, declaring, "The explanation of Harlem's almost secret language is authentic! The incidents are as true to life as modern history! The story is dynamite!" The Avon edition includes "A Note by the Author" in which Van Vechten reasserts his racial authority by highlighting his personal connections to many Harlemites and underscoring the approval of his friends James Weldon Johnson and George S. Schuyler.

Just as Van Vechten's interest in black culture predated *Nigger Heaven,* it lasted long after the novel's controversy died down. Once his medium of choice shifted from prose to photography, his portraits of black Americans created an authoritative catalogue of talent. Most of the writers, musicians, and performers Van Vechten invited to sit before his camera had barely launched their careers when he photographed them—and that so many of them went on to achieve great fame not only testifies to his intimacy with Harlem's artistic ferment but also underscores his ability to identify their promise early. But arguably Van Vechten's most impressive contribution to African American scholarship was his founding of—and tireless work toward—a memorial collection of African American arts and letters at Yale, named for James Weldon Johnson. Van Vechten's dedication to honoring the memory of his dear friend led the inveterate collector to donate his own personal corpus of materials relating to black arts and letters, and his considerable library formed the core of what has since become one of the country's most important collections.

Nigger Heaven has been out of print since Harper and Row's 1971 paperback and a hardcover 1973 reprint by Octagon Books. Even when the novel was out of print, energetic critical reaction to it continued unabated. Many critics persist in challenging Van Vechten's right to write such a book in the first place, and many responses to the novel reflect outrage at his presumption in doing so. Arguing that Van Vechten was motivated by "a mixture of commercialism and patronizing sympathy," David Levering Lewis charges that from "the point of view of racial uplift, *Nigger Heaven* was a colossal fraud in which the depiction of the Talented Tenth in high baroque barely muffled the throb of the tom-tom."[52] While many critics acknowledge Van Vechten's efforts to promote developing black writers, they maintain a response to the novel which is at best skeptical and at worst, downright hostile. John Cooley, for instance, lauds how Van Vechten "brought writers of both races together, striving to overcome prejudice and misunderstanding" while simultaneously insisting that *Nigger Heaven* "was perfectly packaged for that insatiable white appetite in the 1920's—for anything black and primitive."[53] Robert G. O'Meally goes farther, charging that Van Vechten's writings "make clear that he never gave up the cliché image of blacks as a naturally arty and primitive people whose 'savage' qualities of spontaneity, zest for life, moon-timed tardiness, free sex and instinctive good humor were their great gifts."[54] The vituperative tone to which Van Vechten's novel continues to drive critics demonstrates its continued political resonance.

Werner Sollors warns us against such arbitrarily exclusive responses to literature as those which resist *Nigger Heaven* because of Van Vechten's whiteness. "The dominant assumption among serious scholars who study ethnic literary history," he notes, "seems to be that history can best be written by separating the groups that produced such literature in the U.S."[55] And indeed, Van Vechten's biographer Bruce Kellner has made clear that despite *Nigger Heaven*'s "limitations, the novel strengthened Van Vechten's ties with the race and increased his loyalty."[56] Moreover, Kellner notes, Van Vechten himself never used the term "primitive," the one adjective which, ironically, is most often hurled at him by hostile critics. Chidi Ikonne's analysis of the period wisely notes that "the impact (good or bad) of *Nigger Heaven* on the trend of the Harlem Renaissance literature is often blown out of proportion" and argues that "Van Vechten did not initiate the Harlem Renaissance literary trend. He only fostered its receptivity."[57]

Ikonne is correct, I believe, in observing that "*Nigger Heaven* deserves a better treatment than it has received so far."[58] This reissue provides students and scholars alike with an opportunity to review the evolution of race relations during the past seven decades. It renders vivid images of black culture in the 1920s as it stages the drama of race, illustrating the conflicts of passing and implicitly questioning racial authenticity. For those readers who are able to heed James Weldon Johnson's admonition that "the book and not the title is the thing," this issue of *Nigger Heaven* will raise provocative and worthy questions. Appearing as it does at a time when critics of American and African American literature are developing analyses of the racial hybridity which has always characterized American culture, perhaps this reissue will be received as a site for fruitful inquiry, rather than a text so troubling that it must be burned.

NOTES

For permission to reprint previously published and unpublished materials, I am sincerely grateful to the Carl Van Vechten Papers, Manuscripts and Archives Division, The New York Public Library, Astor, Lenox and Tilden Foundations; and The Yale Collection of American Literature, Beinecke Rare Book and Manuscript Library, Yale University. Michael T. Gilmore first encouraged me to pursue this project and he deserves my warmest thanks. Bruce Kellner, Mark Helbling, and Rebecca Morton offered generous and substantive reviews of the introduction's early versions, and I am also indebted to Nellie McKay and Werner Sollors for their encouragement. I am particularly grateful for valuable conversations with Steve Shively, Patricia Willis, Emily Bernard, and Marcy Jane Knopf. This project has benefited from the wisdom, guidance, and support of many: Karen Hewitt and Pat Hollahan at the University of Illinois Press; my colleagues in the English Department at Oakland University; my friends and former colleagues at Yale University. A Faculty Research Grant from Oakland University financed my travel, as did my parents, who provided food, shelter, and so much more. But this project's greatest debt goes to my colleague, partner, and husband, Todd Estes: he has believed in me since before we met; offered me a model for scholarship with integrity, grace, and moral purpose; and he brought me Elizabeth, in all her sweetness and light.

1. Edna Thomas to Carl Van Vechten, 16 August 1926, Carl Van Vechten Papers, Manuscripts and Archives Division, New York Public Library (hereafter Carl Van Vechten Papers).

2. Alain Locke to Carl Van Vechten, 9 February 1926, Carl Van Vechten Papers.

3. Notes for Nigger Heaven, James Weldon Johnson Collection, Yale Collection of American Literature, Beinecke Rare Book and Manuscript Library, Yale University (hereafter James Weldon Johnson Collection).

4. Quoted in Bruce Kellner, ed., *"Keep A-Inchin' Along": Selected Writings of Carl Van Vechten about Black Arts and Letters* (Westport, Conn.: Greenwood Press, 1979), 73.

5. Charles Scruggs, "Crab Antics and Jacob's Ladder: Aaron Douglas's

Two Views of *Nigger Heaven*," in *The Harlem Renaissance Re-Examined,* ed. Victor A. Kramer (New York: AMS Press, 1987), 162.

6. W. E. B. Du Bois, review of *Nigger Heaven* by Carl Van Vechten, *Crisis,* December 1926: 81. The subsequent private amity between Du Bois and Van Vechten has, however, gone largely unnoticed. Van Vechten noted that his first meeting with Du Bois after the latter's "dirty attack on the book" took place at a party given by A'Leila Walker at her studio, where the two "chatted amiably." Later, the author elaborated on the meeting, explaining that a black woman friend (perhaps Walker herself) put him alone in a room with the man who wrote "a terrible review" of the novel, telling them she "thought you two ought to know each other better." Van Vechten explains, "So I respected this man a great deal and we became good friends. I guess he thought maybe white people shouldn't say anything at all about Negroes." See Carl Van Vechten, 30 November 1926, Daybooks, Carl Van Vechten Papers; see also Carl Van Vechten, typescript of interview by William Ingersoll for the Oral History Collection, Columbia University, 3 March 1960, 214.

7. Charles Duane Van Vechten to Carl Van Vechten, 7 December 1925, Carl Van Vechten Papers.

8. Carl Van Vechten, typescript of interview by William Ingersoll, Oral History, 208.

9. Bruce Kellner, *Carl Van Vechten and the Irreverent Decades* (Norman: University of Oklahoma Press, 1968), 220.

10. Quoted in Jervis Anderson, *This Was Harlem* (New York: Farrar Straus Giroux, 1981), 222.

11. W. E. B. Du Bois, "Criteria of Negro Art," in *The Portable Harlem Renaissance Reader,* ed. David Levering Lewis (New York: Viking, 1994), 103.

12. Ibid., 102.

13. Notes and Suggestions Made by Various Authors Concerning Carl Van Vechten's *Nigger Heaven,* James Weldon Johnson Collection.

14. Mrs. William (Alice) Clark Meade to Carl Van Vechten, 27 July 1926, Carl Van Vechten Papers.

15. Charles Johnson to Carl Van Vechten, 10 August 1926, Carl Van Vechten Papers.

16. Langston Hughes, *The Big Sea* (1940; reprint, New York: Thunder's Mouth, 1986), 268.

17. James Weldon Johnson, *Along This Way* (1933; reprint, New York: Penguin, 1990), 382.

18. Carl Van Vechten, typescript of interview by William Ingersoll, Oral History, 15.

19. Carl Van Vechten, "Folksongs of the American Negro," in *"Keep A-Inchin' Along,"* 40.

20. Van Vechten embroidered this story a bit. For a fuller account of the actual chronology of his meeting with Stein, see Edward Burns, "Appendix A: The First Meeting of Gertrude Stein and Carl Van Vechten" in *The Letters of Gertrude Stein and Carl Van Vechten,* ed. Edward Burns, 2 vols. (New York: Columbia University Press, 1986), 2:847–53.

21. Carl Van Vechten to Gertrude Stein, 15 November 1924, in *Letters of Gertrude Stein and Carl Van Vechten,* 1:108.

22. Carl Van Vechten, typescript of interview by William Ingersoll, Oral History, 197.

23. Ibid., 337.

24. Carl Van Vechten, "Moanin' Wid a Sword in Mah Han'," in *"Keep A-Inchin' Along,"* 58.

25. Carl Van Vechten, "Uncle Tom's Mansion," in *"Keep A-Inchin' Along,"* 61.

26. Carl Van Vechten, typescript of interview by William Ingersoll, Oral History, 19.

27. Carl Van Vechten to Fania Marinoff, 10 June 1925, Carl Van Vechten Papers.

28. Carl Van Vechten, Notes for *Nigger Heaven,* Yale Collection of American Literature, Beinecke Rare Book and Manuscript Library, Yale University.

29. Alain Locke, "The Negro Takes His Place in American Art," in *The Portable Harlem Renaissance Reader,* ed. David Levering Lewis (New York: Viking, 1994), 137.

30. Mark Helbling, "Carl Van Vechten and the Harlem Renaissance," *Negro American Literature Forum* 10 (Summer 1976): 39–47.

31. Carl Van Vechten to Gertrude Stein, 30 June 1925, in *Letters of Gertrude Stein and Carl Van Vechten,* 1:116.

32. Carl Van Vechten to Langston Hughes, c. May 1925, James Weldon Johnson Collection.

33. Carl Van Vechten to Fania Marinoff, 3 May 1925, Carl Van Vechten Papers.

34. Carl Van Vechten to Langston Hughes, 5 September 1925, James Weldon Johnson Collection.

35. Carl Van Vechten, Notes for *Nigger Heaven,* Yale Collection of American Literature, Beinecke Rare Book and Manuscript Library, Yale University.

36. James Weldon Johnson, Notes and Suggestions Made by Various Authors Concerning Carl Van Vechten's *Nigger Heaven,* James Weldon Johnson Collection.

37. Carl Van Vechten, 16 May 1926, Daybooks, Carl Van Vechten Papers; Rudolph Fisher, Notes and Suggestions Made by Various Authors Concerning Carl Van Vechten's *Nigger Heaven,* James Weldon Johnson Collection.

38. Carl Van Vechten to Langston Hughes, c. 1925, James Weldon Johnson Collection.

39. Hughes's talent is evident even in these hastily composed lines, though they are generally not included in anthologies of Hughes's work. For a more detailed account, see Bruce Kellner, "Langston Hughes's *Nigger Heaven* Blues," *Langston Hughes Review* 11 (Spring 1992): 21–27.

40. James Weldon Johnson, Notes and Suggestions Made by Various Authors Concerning Carl Van Vechten's *Nigger Heaven,* James Weldon Johnson Collection. Bruce Kellner's account offers even greater detail. See *"Keep A-Inchin' Along,"* 73–74.

41. Nora Holt to Carl Van Vechten, 17 August 1926, Carl Van Vechten Papers.

42. Taylor Gordon to Carl Van Vechten, 16 August 1926, Carl Van Vechten Papers.

43. Charles Johnson to Carl Van Vechten, 10 August 1926, Carl Van Vechten Papers.

44. Charles Chesnutt to Carl Van Vechten, 7 September 1926, James Weldon Johnson Collection.

45. Eric Walrond to Carl Van Vechten, 8 August 1926, Carl Van Vechten Papers.

46. Paul Robeson to Carl Van Vechten, 12 August 1926, Carl Van Vechten Papers.

47. James Weldon Johnson, "Romance and Tragedy in Harlem—A Review," *Opportunity* 4 (October 1926): 316, 330.

48. Arthur Spingarn to Carl Van Vechten, 3 September 1926, Carl Van Vechten Papers.

49. Walter White to Carl Van Vechten, 19 August 1926, Carl Van Vechten Papers.

50. Charles Johnson to Carl Van Vechten, 10 August 1926, Carl Van Vechten Papers; Nella Larsen Imes to Carl Van Vechten, 11 August 1926, Carl Van Vechten Papers.

51. Avery Hopwood to Carl Van Vechten, 22 September 1926, Carl Van Vechten Papers.

52. David Levering Lewis, *When Harlem Was in Vogue* (New York: Oxford University Press, 1981), 188.

53. John Cooley, "White Writers and the Harlem Renaissance," in *The Harlem Renaissance: Revaluations*, ed. Amritjit Singh, William S. Shiver, and Stanley Brodwin (New York: Garland Press, 1989), 20.

54. Robert G. O'Meally, "Harlem Renaissance Man," *Times Literary Supplement*, 30 September 1988: 1066.

55. Werner Sollors, "A Critique of Pure Pluralism," in *Reconstructing American Literary History*, ed. Sacvan Bercovitch (Cambridge: Harvard University Press, 1986), 255.

56. Bruce Kellner, "Carl Van Vechten's Black Renaissance," in *The Harlem Renaissance: Revaluations*, ed. Amritjit Singh, William S. Shiver and Stanley Brodwin (New York: Garland Press, 1989), 31.

57. Chidi Ikonne, *From Du Bois to Van Vechten: The Early Negro Literature* (Westport, Conn.: Greenwood Press, 1981), 37, 38.

58. Ibid., 36.

Nigger Heaven

PROLOGUE

Prologue

Anatole Longfellow, alias the Scarlet Creeper,[1] strutted aimfully down the east side of Seventh Avenue. He wore a tight-fitting suit of shepherd's plaid which thoroughly revealed his lithe, sinewy figure to all who gazed upon him, and all gazed. A great diamond, or some less valuable stone which aped a diamond, glistened in his fuchsia cravat. The uppers of his highly polished tan boots were dove-coloured suède and the buttons were pale blue. His black hair was sleek under his straw hat, set at a jaunty angle. When he saluted a friend—and his acquaintanceship seemed to be wide—two rows of pearly teeth gleamed from his seal-brown countenance.

It was the hour when promenading was popular—about eleven o'clock in the evening. The air was warm, balmy for June, and not too humid. Over the broad avenue, up and down which multi-hued taxicabs rolled, hung a canopy of indigo sky, spangled with bright stars. The shops, still open, were brilliantly illuminated. Slouching under the protecting walls of the buildings, in front of show-windows, or under the trees, groups of young men

[1] The reader will find, at the end of this volume, a glossary of the unusual Negro words and phrases employed in this novel.

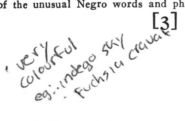

congregated, chattering and laughing. Women, in pairs, or with male escorts, strolled up and down the ample sidewalk.

Hello, 'Toly! A stalwart black man accosted the Creeper.

Hello, Ed. How you been?

Po'ly, thank you. How *you* been?

No complaints. Nummer come out. Drew sixty-seven bucks.

Holy Kerist!

Yeh. Anatole displayed his teeth.

What nummer?

Seven-Nine-Eight.

Whah you found et?

Off'n a gal's fron' do'.

Comin' out?

Goin' in. Ah went out duh back winder. Her daddy done come home widout writin'.

Hush mah mouf!

Ah doan mean mebbe.

As Anatole walked on, his self-esteem flowered. Unbuttoning his coat, he expanded his chest, dangerously stretching the gold watch-chain which extended from pocket to pocket across his muscular belly.

Howdy.

Howdy.

He greeted in passing Leanshanks Pescod, a mulatto lightweight who, in successive Saturday sessions at the Commonwealth Club, had defeated two white comers.

Is you enjoyin' de air, Mr. Longfellow?

'Deed, Ah is, Mrs. Guckeen. How you been? The Creeper's manner became slightly flirtatious.

Thank you, Mr. Longfellow, an' pretty well.

Mrs. Imogene Guckeen was the proprietor of a popular beauty parlour further up the avenue. It was Anatole's custom to indulge in a manicure at this parlour every afternoon around five. As a wide circle of admiring women was cognizant of this habit, five was the rush hour at Mrs. Guckeen's establishment. She was fully aware of the important rôle this customer played in her affairs and, as a consequence, made no effort to collect his always considerable bill. Occasionally, moreover, the Creeper would slip her five or ten dollars on account, adding a chuck under her drooping chin and a devastating smile.

Turning about at One hundred and twenty-seventh Street, Anatole faced north and resumed his leisurely promenade. Now, however, despite the apparently careless flipping and twisting of his ebony cane, tipped with a ball of ivory, his air was more serious. He peered into the faces of the women he encountered with an expression that was almost anxious. Once, so eagerly did he seek a pair of eyes which obstinately refused to return his stare, he bumped into an elderly black man with a long white beard, who limped, supported by a cane. Anatole caught the old fellow only in time to prevent his falling.

Ah sartainly beg yo' pahdon, he said with his most enchanting smile.

The octogenarian returned the smile.

'Pears to me, he squeaked, dat you's mos' unnacherly perlite fo' dis street at dis hour.

The Creeper's breast expanded a full two inches, causing his watch-chain, stretched to capacity, to drag a ring of jangling keys from his waistcoat pocket. Replacing the keys, he reflected that he could afford to be agreeable, even magnanimous, to harmless old gentlemen. Was there another sheik in Harlem who possessed one-tenth his attraction for the female sex? Was there another of whose muscles the brick-pressers, ordinarily quite free with their audible, unflattering comments about passers-by, were more afraid? As he meditated in this wise, his pride received an unexpected jolt. Under the bright lights in front of the Lafayette Theatre, he discerned a pompous figure whose presence obliterated the smug cheerfulness from his heart.

A few years earlier Randolph Pettijohn had made his start in Harlem as a merchant of hot-dogs. His little one-storey shop, hugged between two towering buildings, had rapidly become popular. His frankfurters were excellent; his buns were fresh; his mustard beyond reproach. In a short time Pettijohn's business was so successful, the overhead expense so light—he was his own cook and he personally served his customers over the counter—that he had saved a sufficient sum of money to invest in real-estate, an investment which increased in value over-night. Next, with the proceeds of a few judicious sales, he opened a cabaret which shortly became the favourite resort in Harlem. Now, his Bolito game had made him so rich that his powerfully exerted influence began to be felt in political circles.

Unreasoningly, Anatole hated him. He had never inimically crossed the Creeper's path, but somehow, subconsciously, Anatole was aware that such an eventuality was by no means impossible. Besides, it irked the Creeper to realize that any one else possessed power of whatever kind. The feeling was not reciprocated. Anatole was frequently a spectacular figure at the Winter Palace, Pettijohn's cabaret, where he was welcome because he was known to be a particular favourite with jig-chasers from below the line.

How you been, 'Toly? The Bolito King greeted the Creeper warmly, even affectionately.

Hello, Ran.

Lookin' 'em over?

Ah'm takin' 'em in. The Creeper was reticent.

You sartainly are one dressin' up fool, Creeper, one of the King's companions inserted.

Heavy lover, too, another added.

The King offered his accolade: Nobody like

duh Creeper fo' close an' women, nobody a-tall.

Anatole exposed his pearls. Bottle et, he suggested.

Come in an' see me, Pettijohn invited. Mah Winter Palace is open winter an' summer.

Completely at his ease again, the Creeper strutted on, swinging his cane, expanding his chest, and humming to himself:

> Mah man's got teeth lak a lighthouse on duh sea,
> An' when he smiles he throws dem lights on me.

Howdy, 'Toly!

As Anatole looked into the unwelcome eyes of a high yellow boy whose suit was shiny and whose boots were patched, his manner became a trifle patronizing.

How you been, Duke?

Not so good, 'Toly. Duh show done went broke.

Dere'll be annudder.

Sho'. How's Ah gwine live till den?

The Creeper proffered no advice.

You lookin' mighty lucky, 'Toly. The Duke's tone was one of whining admiration.

The Creeper preserved his discreet silence.

Ah nebber did see no sheik what had yo' gif' fo' dressin'.

The Creeper's chest was the thermometer of the effect of this compliment.

Ah's hungry, 'Toly. Hones'. Gimme duh price of a dog.

Drawing a handful of loose change from his trouser-pocket, with great deliberation the Creeper selected a quarter from this heap and passed it to his indigent acquaintance.

Heah you is, Duke. . . . He had the air of a munificent benefactor. . . . Now why ain' you git mo' providen'?

Ah is, 'Toly, when Ah gits duh chance. 'T'ain' mah fault duh show done went broke. Inserting the quarter in his mouth, the boy made a sudden dash down a side-street.

Han' full o' gimme, mouf full o' much oblige, mused the Creeper.

At the corner of One hundred and thirty-seventh Street, surrounded by a numerous group of spectators, many of whom clapped their hands rhythmically, a crowd of urchins executed the Charleston. Apparently without intent, Anatole joined these pleasure-seekers. His eyes, however, quickly shifted from the dancers and stole around the ring of onlookers, in hasty but accurate inspection. Suddenly he found that for which he had been searching.

She was a golden-brown and her skin was clear, as soft as velvet. As pretty a piece, he reflected, as he had seen around these parts for some time, and he had not happened to see her before. Her slender body was encased in coral silk, the skirt sufficiently short to expose her trim legs in golden-brown stockings. A turquoise-blue cloche all but covered her straight black shingled hair. Her soft, brown eyes seemed to be begging. Withdrawing his own gaze almost immediately, so swift had been his satisfactory appraisal, he was nevertheless aware that she was contriving, without appearing to do so, without, indeed, appearing to look at him at all, to edge nearer to him. Never once, while she carried out her design, did her hands refrain from the rhythmic clapping which accompanied the juvenile dancers. When at last, she stood by his side, so close that he might touch her, she continued to pretend that she was only interested in the intricate steps of the Charleston. Anatole, outwardly, gave no sign whatever that he was aware of her presence.

After they had played this game of mutual duplicity for some time, she, losing patience or acquiring courage, accosted him.

Hello, 'Toly.

He turned, without a smile, and stared at her.

Ah doan seem to recerllec' dat Ah got duh honour o' yo' acquaintance.

You ain', Mr. 'Toly, an' dat's a fac'. Mah name's Ruby.

He did not encourage her to proceed.

Ruby Silver, she completed.

He remained silent. Presently, in an offhand way, he began to clap his hands. A particularly agile lad of six was executing some pretty capers. Hey! Hey! Do that thing!

Everybody knows who you is, Mr. 'Toly, *every-body!* Her voice implored his attention.

The Creeper continued to clap.

Ah been jes' nacherly crazy to meet you.

The Creeper was stern. What fo'? he shot out.

You knows, Mr. 'Toly. I guess you knows.

He drew her a little apart from the ring.

How much you got?

Oh, Ah been full o' prosperity dis evenin'. Ah met an ofay wanted to change his luck. He gimme a tenner.

The Creeper appeared to be taking the matter under consideration. Ah met a gal las' night dat offer me fifteen, he countered. Nevertheless, it could be seen that he was weakening.

Ah got annuder five in mah lef' stockin', an' Ah'll show you lovin' such as you never seen.

The Creeper became more affable. Ah do seem to remember yo' face, Miss Silver, he averred. Will you do me duh favour to cling to mah arm.

As they strolled, their bodies touching, down a dark side-street, his hand freely explored her flesh, soft and warm under the thin covering of coral silk.

Wanna dance? he demanded.

Luvvit, she replied.

Come across.

She stooped to fumble in her stockings, first the right, then the left. Presently she handed him two bills which he stuffed into his waistcoat pocket without the formality of examination.

Winter Palace? she inquired.

A nasty shadow flitted across Anatole's face.

Naw, he retorted. Too many ofays an' jigchasers.

Bowie Wilcox's is dicty.

Too many monks.

Atlantic City Joe's?

Too many pink-chasers an' bulldikers.

Where den?

Duh Black Venus.

A few moments later they were swallowed by an entrance on Lenox Avenue, flanked by two revolving green lights. Arm in arm, they descended the stairs to the basement. As they walked down the long hallway which led to the dance-floor, the sensual blare of jazz, slow, wailing jazz, stroked their ears. At the door three waiters in evening clothes greeted the Creeper with enthusiasm.

Why, dat's sartainly Mr. 'Toly.

Good evenin'.

Gwine sit at mah table?

Mine?

Mine, Mr. 'Toly?

Expanding his chest, Anatole gazed down the length of the hall. Couples were dancing in such close proximity that their bodies melted together as they swayed and rocked to the tormented howling of the brass, the barbaric beating of the drum. Across each woman's back, clasped tight against her shoulder blades, the black hands of her partner were flattened. Blues, smokes, dinges, charcoals, chocolate browns, shines, and jigs.

Le's hoof, Ruby urged.

Le's set down, Anatole commanded. Passing his straw hat to the hat-check girl, he followed a waiter to an empty table, pushing Ruby ahead of him.

Hello, 'Toly! A friend hailed him from an adjoining table.

Hello, Licey.

A pint, the Creeper ordered.

The waiter Charlestoned down the floor to the intoxicating rhythm, twirling his tray on palm held high overhead.

Put ashes in sweet papa's bed so as he can' slip out, moaned Licey in the Creeper's ear. Ah knows a lady what'll be singing, Wonder whah mah easy rider's gone!

Bottle et.

Licey chuckled. Hush mah mouf ef Ah doan!

The waiter came back, like a cat, shuffling ingeniously from one side of the room to the other, in and out of the throng of dancers. Charleston! Charleston! Do that thing! Oh boy!

On his tray were two glasses, two splits of ginger ale, and a bowl of cracked ice. From his hip-pocket he extracted a bottle containing a transparent liquid. He poured out the ginger ale. Anatole poured out the gin.

Tea fo' two! he toasted his companion, almost jovially.

She gulped her glassful in one swallow, and then giggled, 'Toly, you's mah sho' 'nough daddy an' Ah sho' does love you wid all mah h'aht.

Everybody loves mah baby, tooted the cornet.

But mah baby doan love nobody but me, Ruby chimed in. She tentatively touched the Creeper's arm. As he did not appear to object to this attention, she stroked it tenderly.

Jes' once 'roun', she pleaded.

He humoured her. Embracing her closely, he rocked her slowly around the hall. Their heels shuffled along the floor. Their knees clicked amorously. On all sides of the swaying couple, bodies in picturesque costumes rocked, black bodies, brown bodies, high yellows, a kaleidoscope of colour transfigured by the amber searchlight. Scarves of bottle green, cerise, amethyst, vermilion, lemon. The drummer in complete abandon tossed his sticks in the air while he shook his head like a wild animal. The saxophone player drew a dilapidated derby over the bowl of his instrument, smothering the din. The banjos planked deliriously. The band snored and snorted and whistled and laughed like a hyena. This music reminded the Creeper of the days when he worked as a bootblack in a Memphis barbershop. Hugged closely together, the bodies rocked and swayed, rocked and swayed. Sometimes a rolling-eyed couple, caught in the whirlpool of aching sound, would scarcely move from one spot. Then the floor-manager would cry, Git off dat dime!

Unexpectedly it was over. The saxophone player substituted the stub of a black cigar for the tube of his instrument. As if they had been released from some subtle enchantment the dancing couples broke apart, dazed, and lumbered towards their tables. Now that music was lacking their bodies had lost the secret of the magic rhythm. Normal illumination. A new mood. Laughter and chatter. A woman shrieked hysterically. The Creeper drew the bottle from his hip-pocket and poured out two more drinks.

Again Ruby drained her portion at one gulp. This time she had repudiated the ginger ale. Again she caressed her companion's arm. Again she sought his eyes, his great brown eyes, like a doe's.

Ah sho' will show you some lovin', daddy, she promised.

The Creeper grunted his approval.

Does you know what Ah calls dis? she continued rapturously.

Calls what?

Dis place, where Ah met you—Harlem. Ah calls et, specherly tonight, Ah calls et Nigger Heaven! I jes' nacherly think dis heah is Nigger Heaven!

On the floor a scrawny yellow girl in pink silk, embroidered with bronze sequins in floral designs, began to sing:

> Mah daddy rocks me with one steady roll;
> Dere ain' no slippin' when he once takes hol' . . .

The Creeper sipped his gin meditatively.

BOOK ONE

MARY

One

Mary Love closed the door softly behind her, shutting out the brassy blare of the band playing on the floor below, crossed the room, and hesitated before the open window. Unwontedly, she found herself quite ready to cry and she welcomed the salt breeze that blew in from the ocean. When she had consented to spend the week-end with Adora Boniface she had not taken into consideration, she discovered, all that this acceptance would imply. She had met—she should have known that she would meet—people who, on the whole, were not her kind. Adora, in her earlier life on the stage, and in her later rich marriage, had gathered about her—and tolerated—a set which included individuals who would never have been admitted into certain respectable homes in Harlem. There was, for example, Randolph Pettijohn, the Bolito King. Adora had probably invited him because he was rich and good-natured. Mary conceded the affluence and the good-nature. She even tried not to be a snob when she thought of the manner in which he had accumulated his fortune. Hot-dogs, cabarets, even gambling, all served their purposes in life, no doubt, although the game of Numbers was a deliberate—and somewhat heartless, considering the average winnings—appeal to a weakness in the ignorant members of her race which she could not readily condone. It was not, however, Pettijohn's background which had won Mary's disfavour. Rather, it was his unpleasant habit of stopping her on the landings of the staircases, of pursuing her into the secluded nooks of the garden, behind the fir hedges. Mary's past experience had not been of a nature to fit her to cope easily with these unwelcome advances. Even now, she was perturbed by the reflection that Randolph might dare follow her into Adora's bedroom.

There was, she could perceive, nothing in Adora's attitude, nothing in the attitude of the house-party as a group, which would indicate that any one regarded such conduct with disapproval. Sylvia Hawthorne obviously had come expressly for the purpose of carrying on her more or less clandestine affair with Rumsey Meadows under auspices which would not too completely compromise her either in the eyes of her husband or the eyes of the more formal Harlem world to which she belonged. The others slipped about a good deal in pairs. If you passed a chamber in which two were sitting, you were likely to hear no words spoken. As for Adora herself, it was clear that she had settled her ephemeral fancy on Alcester Parker, but somehow Mary felt that she could forgive Adora anything.

Mary had known all about Adora, and liked her

in spite of all she knew, for a long time. Adora's former superior position on the stage, rare for one of her race in the early twentieth century, had awarded her a secure situation even before she married the wealthy real-estate dealer who, through rises in value of Harlem property, had been enabled to turn over to his widow at his death an estate which had few serious rivals in the new community. Frowned upon in many quarters, not actually accepted intimately in others—not accepted in any sense of the word, of course, by the old and exclusive Brooklyn set—Adora nevertheless was a figure not to be ignored. She was too rich, too important, too influential, for that. To be sure, she had never been conspicuous for benefactions to her race. On the other hand, she could be counted on for occasional splurges when a hospital was in need of an endowment or when a riot in some city demanded a call for a defence fund. Also, she was undeniably warm-hearted, amusing, in her outspoken way, and even beautiful, in a queenly African manner that set her apart from the other beauties of her race whose loveliness was more frequently of a Latin than an Ethiopian character. It was her good heart, together with her ready wit, that had won Mary as an adherent, with the additional fact that it suited Adora to be agreeable to Mary. Mary, consequently, really liked her, and often made it a point to seek her out for a chat at one or another of the large parties in Harlem where they met. It was quite reasonable then, when, last week, Adora, encountering Mary in a Lenox Avenue music-shop, remarked that she looked peaked, that too close confinement in the library where she worked was not good for her health, invited her to spend a week-end at her country place on Long Island, for Mary to accept the invitation not only gratefully, but even with alacrity.

She recalled now, however, that certain of her friends, without saying very much, had suggested, perhaps with looks rather than words, that she might find the experiment distasteful. However that might be, Mary, her word once given, had kept it.

She had been here since Friday. It was now Sunday afternoon and several automobiles full of late arrivals had been welcomed with a dance, for which a celebrated jazz-band had been imported from New York. These late-comers had done nothing to dispel the atmosphere of the previous days. Rather, they had enhanced it. One party which had driven down in a great Packard announced its advent by tossing sundry empty gin bottles out into the drive. Another case of this favourite beverage, however, had immediately been opened in their honour. Gin, indeed, flowed as freely as if there had been a natural spring of it, while whisky, Scotch, rye, and Bourbon, was almost equally plentiful. So the petting continued, petting which, in some instances, with the amount of evidence under her eyes, seemed to

Mary something which might be called by an uglier name. There were, to be sure, sporadic parties at bridge or pinocle at little tables in several of the rooms in the spacious house, but after a time these were certain to end in a row about money or the desire on the part of some of the gamblers to return to the delights of amorous embraces.

Mary tried to feel that she was not a prig. She tried to assure herself that she might herself enjoy such attentions under more favourable circumstances. She tried to explain to herself that she was selective and not an exhibitionist. However that might be, she was obliged to confess that she was thoroughly out of harmony with her present environment.

At any rate, she mused, it's nobody's fault but my own. I should have had sense enough not to come. Anyway I won't be rude. I suppose I can manage to evade that old satyr for another sixteen hours without being silly or screaming for help—the others would only laugh, in any case, if I did that—and tomorrow I'll be back in my room in Harlem, just as poor as ever, but, thank God, a trifle more intelligent. I won't do just this again in a hurry.

She shook off her sombre mood, almost with a conscious movement of her shoulders, determining to think of impersonal matters. After all, she decided, with a kind of voluntary optimism, the view from this window is superb. In a pool below, shadowed by weeping-willow-trees with spreading boughs which swept the lawn, yellow water-lilies floated and rose lotus blooms nodded on their long, graceful stalks. Beyond, between the trees, across a green sward, lay the sea in which, taking advantage of the splendour of the day, several men were bathing. Two or three of them lay recumbent on the sand, their brown limbs gleaming like bronze in the sun. Others splashed about in the water. Now a youth was mounting the tower in preparation for a dive. He was, she noted, slightly lighter in colour than the others, almost the shade of coffee diluted with rich cream, her preferred tint. At the top of the tower he paused for an instant, arms high over head, long enough for her to catch the symmetrical proportions of his body, the exquisite form of his head, emphasized by his closely cropped, curly, black hair. Now, in a wide, parabolic curve, he dived, cut the water with his hands, and disappeared. Mary emitted an involuntary cry of pleasure: the action was so perfect; *thrilling,* she defined it. It was repeated many times, varied with much laughter and splashing below, and then the young man ran rapidly up the beach and vanished in the bath-house.

Mary turned away from the window and faced the room. Her discontent—disapproval would be a more just word—had vanished. She felt warmer, more understanding and sympathetic. The chamber itself she now found grateful to her eyes, suited to her mood. It was hung in peach-coloured taffeta, expertly draped, the folds held in place by silver coronets, surmounted by plumes of a delicate blue. The bed, innocent of upright pieces, was merely a broad couch hidden beneath a covering of tiger-skins from under which peeped the supports created in the guise of griffins' claws. Magenta and silver cushions were scattered over its expanse. The rest of the furniture was a heavy Bavarian version of Empire, upholstered in dove-hued damask, the arms of the chairs terminating in silver swans' heads. Mary's roving glance included the dressing-table, beneath its canopy of taffeta, laid out with brushes and combs and boxes of tortoise-shell, rows of crystal, ruby, and sapphire bottles and vials, and tiny enamelled receptacles containing rouges and ointments. Loving luxury, all this panoply appealed to Mary's senses, awarded her, in itself, a definite happiness. Had she been alone in this house with Adora, she would have had, she was beginning to believe, a perfect time.

She crossed the room and stood before the dressing-table, regarding her reflection in the mirror, a mirror blessed and consecrated by two hovering silver Cupids. The attentions of Randolph Pettijohn had not augmented her vanity, but she was not displeased by her double. The rich golden-brown colour of her skin was well set off by the simple frock of Pompeian-red crêpe which she wore. Her features were regular, her brown eyes unusually rich. Her hair, parted and smoothed over her forehead, was caught in a low knot just above the nape of her neck. She could not, justifiably, complain about her appearance. Her expression, too, she recognized with pleasure, was lighter, more carefree. What a fool I have been, she assured herself, not to enjoy all this, not to take it for what it is! I may never again be surrounded by such beauty. Mary sighed.

She turned, as she heard the unfastening of the door, to see Adora enter, a languid, fatigued Adora, supported on the one side by Piqua St. Paris, on the other by Arabia Scribner. The group resembled, Mary thought afterwards, Cleopatra, guided by Charmian and Iras.

Perceiving the room to be already occupied, Adora regained a little of her spent vitality.

Why, Mary, she exclaimed, we've missed you. What are you doing off here, all by yourself?

I was tired, Mary explained, and I came up here because you can see the garden better from this window.

I'm tired too, Adora sighed, sinking into a fauteuil, tired to death of all those Niggers [1] downstairs. Sometimes I hate Niggers.

Adora dear, chirped Mrs. St. Paris, in a shrill,

[1] While this informal epithet is freely used by Negroes among themselves, not only as a term of opprobrium, but also actually as a term of endearment, its employment by a white person is always fiercely resented. The word Negress is forbidden under all circumstances.

sycophantic tone, can't I find something to cover your knees? Looking about she sighted a lemon-yellow dressing-gown hanging over a Coromandel screen. Gathering it in her arms, she spread it over her idol's limbs.

My knees are all right, Adora whined. It's my feet. . . .

Mrs. Scribner was on the floor at once, removing the offending satin shoes.

My feet . . . and those damn Niggers.

Silently, Mary applauded this sentiment.

It isn't you, Mary dear—in making this reservation Adora disregarded the presence of the other two ladies—it isn't you. It's that ink-fingered trash downstairs. Oh, a few of them are all right, but most of them come here to drink my booze and eat my food and raise hell at my expense. If I was poor they wouldn't come near me, not a damn one of them.

Why, Adora, protested Mrs. Scribner, we'd come to you in a hovel.

Um, Adora responded doubtfully, the while she stretched forward her released feet and wriggled her silk-encased toes. Suppose you ring the bell.

Mrs. St. Paris pressed a button in the wall.

Mary was surprised to find herself actually interested in studying Adora. She *was* beautiful, of that there could be no question, beautiful and regal. Her skin was almost black; her nose broad, her lips thick. Her ears were set well on her head;

her head was set well on her shoulders. She was a type of pure African majesty. She was garbed in a pansy chiffon robe which matched the pansy lights in her lustrous eyes. Caught by an invisible chain around her ebony forehead gleamed a single pear-shaped emerald.

As, in response to the summons of the bell, a maid entered, Mary noted what she had often observed before in the expression of dependent Negroes in the homes of rich members of her race, a certain sullen mien. We don't like to wait on each other, she reflected bitterly.

Nellie, Adora ordered, bring up four champagne-glasses and a bowl of ice.

Without responding, without, indeed, giving any indication that she had heard, the maid shuffled out of the room.

Now, where are my mules?

The sycophants in their haste, each to reach the proper closet first, bumped into each other and exchanged glares.

After she had been shod more comfortably, the former music hall star rose majestically and hobbled towards a chest of drawers. From beneath a heap of filmy chiffon and lace she extracted a bunch of keys. Selecting one, she unlocked a cupboard, the shelves of which, Mary observed, were occupied by rows of reclining bottles bundled in straw. Choosing one, Adora returned to the comfort of her armchair.

I need a drink bad, she averred, and nothing but champagne will do. It always cheers me up.

Presently Nellie returned with the glasses and a silver bowl containing ice. Drawing a small coffee-table near her mistress's chair, she placed her burden upon it and retired as silently as she had approached.

Nellie talks about as much as Coolidge, Adora remarked as she cooled the glasses and poured out the wine. The eyes of Mrs. St. Paris and Mrs. Scribner were greedy, but Adora ignored their message.

Mary, she said, here's yours.

Mary drew nearer and accepted the proffered goblet. Now, somewhat grudgingly, Adora served the other two ladies.

Sit down, Mary.

Mary obeyed her.

I like you, Mary, and I'm going to drink to your success.

Oh, yes, the sycophants echoed, to Mary's success!

Without further preliminary the ladies proceeded to sip their wine.

Thank you, Adora, Mary responded, but I haven't a notion what kind of success I want.

There's only one success for a woman, Adora announced, at least for a coloured woman, and that's a good husband, and a good husband for a coloured woman means a rich husband.

I don't know that I want to be married, Mary protested.

Oh, go on! Now what else can a coloured woman do? You're a librarian, but you'll never get as much pay as the white librarians. They won't even put you in charge of a branch library. Not because you're not as good as the others—probably you're better—but because you're coloured. If you were a trained nurse it would be the same. The only chance a coloured woman has—she can't be a doctor or a lawyer or a preacher or a real-estate agent like a man—is on the stage, and you'd be no good on the stage! Why, probably you can't even dance the Charleston!

I can—a little. Mary laughed grimly.

Well, a little isn't enough. Anyway, they don't want your type on the stage any more, or mine either, for that matter. If I wanted to work today I bet I couldn't get a job. The managers, especially the shine managers, are looking for high yallers. Well, I can't say I blame 'em. I'm sick of Niggers myself, damn sick of these black Niggers!

Adora sipped her wine meditatively.

I might open a beauty parlour. Mary essayed a weak attempt at humour.

Yes, you might, but there are forty of those on every street in Harlem already. And you might start another Black Star Line, or peddle snow, or become an undertaker, but you won't do any of these things.

The glasses of Mrs. St. Paris and Mrs. Scribner were conspicuously empty, their expressions eager, their arms all but outstretched. Overlooking this condition, Adora filled her own glass and continued in her rich, steady voice, low and musical, and with the commanding presence she had acquired during her career on the stage: There's an old song which I used to hear when I toured the South: Ain't it hard to be a Nigger? Ever hear it? Without waiting for a reply, Adora lay back in her chair and began to croon:

> Ain't it hard, ain't it hard,
> Ain't it hard to be a Nigger, Nigger, Nigger?
> Ain't it hard, ain't it hard?
> Fo' you can't git yo' money when it's due.

Well, I guess it is, though it partly depends on the way you look at it. It's hard for those who don't face facts. Now, I always do just that. Mary, she went on earnestly, almost pleadingly, I wish you'd get married.

Why, Adora, what can I do if nobody wants me? Mary tried to laugh off her embarrassment.

Well, you know as well as I do there's a certain party round here that's pretty crazy to get you.

Mary regarded her hostess with unfeigned astonishment.

You don't think he wants to *marry* me? she queried, too dumfounded to make any pretence that she was unaware of the identity of the person to whom Adora referred.

In a minute. This afternoon. Neglecting the glasses of her guests—Mary's, as a matter of fact, remained nearly full—she offered herself another libation, whereupon the sycophants scowled.

Mary's conflicting emotions did not permit her to speak at once.

Well, Mary, what do you say?

If you don't mind, Adora. . . . If you don't mind, I'd rather not talk about it.

Nonsense! . . . There came a loud knocking at the door. . . . More of those Niggers! Go see who it is, Piqua, Adora ordered.

It's Ran and Al.

Adora's expression softened. It was even tender. Oh, they can come in, she said.

The fat Bolito King, his smug, brown countenance wreathed in a wrinkled smile, his eyes assisted by a pince-nez, set in gold, entered, followed by a slender tea-coloured youth, in a blue flannel coat, white trousers, and sneakers.

Well, boys, just in time for a little fizz-water, Adora cried.

We was lookin' fo' you an' et, the King admitted.

More particularly for you, Al added.

Well, for that you can both have a drink out of my glass, Adora suggested. Here's yours. She passed the glass to Al who drained the remnant at one gulp. Adora inverted the bottle. Only a few drops trickled out. Get another bottle, Arabia, she commanded, her eyes following Al as he moved towards the window.

The hammering on the portal was repeated.

Let them in, Adora sighed. It's no use trying to be alone in this place. Let them in, but stow away the champagne and bring out the Scotch.

Been looking for you everywhere, Adora, cried Dr. Lister, the handsome and popular young dentist, as the door swung open. Behind him surged Lutie Panola, fat and merry, dressed in violet muslin and resembling an overgrown doll; Sylvia Hawthorne, smart in her shingle-haired, slender, yellow way, in a dress of ecru linen embroidered in bright wools; smiling, smoking a cigarette through an amber holder, she leaned on the arm of Rumsey Meadows; Irwin Latrobe, Lucas Garfield, Guymon Hooker, Carmen Fisher, Hope Rosemount, and finally, the stranger whom Mary had watched diving brought up the rear.

Can we dance in here, 'Dora? Sylvia demanded. We've danced damn near everywhere else.

Her hostess making an impatient gesture of assent, Sylvia set the phonograph which soon was spinning around to the tune of Little Turtle Dove Love!

Roll up the rugs! Sylvia cried.

Rumsey obeyed her and three couples began to dance at once.

Lucas Garfield, who the previous spring had been

leading man in a Negro revue called James Crow, Esquire, imitated the strumming of a ukelele with his fingers while he sang:

> Oh, how I'm aching for love!
> Wish I had a little turtle dove
> To coo, coo, coo to me . . .

Lutie Panola had thrown herself on the bed. She lay, a vast violet muslin heap on the tiger-skin covering, kicking up her heels, shivering like a mammoth platter of jelly, and emitting gurgles of joy. Dr. Lister dragged Mary to the floor and she danced with him willingly enough, only too grateful to escape the attentions of Pettijohn for the time being. Adora was beating time with the heel of her mule, while her two satellites and Alcester Parker waved their arms in rhythm with the music.

When the phonograph ran down, the noise increased. The men sought drinks, the women lipsticks. Mary gravitated towards the open window. Suddenly, through the uproar, in a clear undertone that ripped the din like thunder, she heard a voice behind her which unaccountably made her tremble.

You seem out of place here, if you don't mind my saying so, the voice said.

She turned quickly to face the diver, furious that he, a stranger, should take for granted what she felt to be true.

I don't know what you mean, she protested.

Yes, you do too, he went on imperturbably. La Boniface is all right, but apparently she invites a lot of riff-raff to her parties.

I dare say I'm no better than any one else. She could have bitten her tongue out after she had made this priggish remark. What would he think of her?

I dare say none of us is, he responded. It's just a matter of what we like and what we don't like. Now I don't believe you like *this*.

In drunken despair, Lutie was sobbing now. Lucas, still imitating the ukelele, warbled:

What does it matter that
I want you?
What does it matter that
You want me?
Like a sweet lump of sugar
In a hot cup of tea
Love don't last nohow,
Melts away somehow.
What does it matter that . . .

Wow! screamed Sylvia. Bottle it, Lucas, for cryin' out loud.

Mary smiled. I don't believe I've met you, she said.

My name's Byron Kasson: he introduced himself. I'm just graduated from the University of Pennsylvania. Came out here today with a bunch

I met in New York. Shall I ask some one to introduce you to me?

No, don't. She spoke quickly. She was less nervous now. My name is Mary Love.

Somehow, Miss Love . . . it was his turn to be embarrassed . . . you stand out in a crowd like this. I couldn't help liking you even before I talked to you.

I saw you first . . . diving.

He smiled. That's the only thing I do well.

You do *that* well. Is it your profession?

I haven't any profession yet. I want to write, he went on.

You're a writer! Mary exclaimed with enthusiasm.

Oh, I haven't published much. I've had a piece or two in Opportunity, but that won't keep me alive. At college they said I had promise. I know what they meant, he added, "pretty good for a coloured man." That doesn't satisfy me. I want to be as good as any one. It's frightfully noisy here, he went on. Couldn't we find a quieter spot?

It's noisy all over the place. Downstairs, there's a jazz-band. Anyhow, if we go anywhere else we're sure to be followed. I came up here to get away from the confusion and you can see how successful I've been. Why don't you call on me in New York?

I'm not living in New York. I'm going back to Philadelphia tomorrow. Later, I hope to return.

When?

I don't know. He grinned. You see, I haven't a bean. Got to work at something while I practise writing, and I haven't the faintest notion what I can do.

Interrupted by a terrifying scream, they turned to see Sylvia and Rumsey, one tugging at each ankle, dragging Lutie off the bed. Clinging to the tiger-skin, kicking, shrieking, she fell to the floor.

Here you, be careful of my skins! Adora warned them harshly.

It's all right, 'Dora, Sylvia replied. I'll put it back.

Unwinding the screaming Lutie, Rumsey assisted her to her feet and began to dance with her while he sang ribaldly:

> By an' by,
> By an' by,
> I'm goin' to lay down this heavy load . . .

You bum, you! Lutie pummelled him.

Randolph Pettijohn approached the pair in the window.

Ah doan never seem to fin' no chance to speak to you, Miss Mary, he began.

Byron Kasson turned and walked away. Mary realized that she had no right to stop him.

An' Ah got somethin' to say, an' dere ain' much time lef' to say et in, the King continued. Ah knows Ah ain' yo' kin', but you's mine. Ah wants a nice, 'spectable 'ooman for a wife . . . Mary opened her mouth to speak . . . Wait a minute. Ah ain't elegant. Ah ain' got no eddication lak you, but Ah got money, plenty of et, an' Ah got love. Ah'd mek you happy an' you'd give me what Ah wants, a 'spectable 'ooman. Ef you want to, we'd live on Strivers' Row . . .

At last Mary succeeded in stopping him. I'm sorry, Mr. Pettijohn, she said, but it's no use. You see, I don't love you.

Dat doan mek no difference, he whispered softly. Lemme mek you.

I'm afraid it's impossible, Mary asserted more firmly.

The Bolito King regarded her fixedly and with some wonder. You cain' mean no, he said. Ah's willin' to wait, an' to wait some time, but Ah gotta git you. You jes' what Ah desires.

It's impossible, Mary repeated sternly, as she turned away.

The room had now become pandemonium. Singly and in couples the crowd danced the Black Bottom and the Charleston. The phonograph was kept incessantly active. Drinks were poured out lavishly. Guymon Hooker, indeed, playfully emptied a bottle of Scotch through an open window. At last, apparently, Adora had had all she could stand.

Rising, she pointed her finger towards the door.

Get out of here, the whole pack of you! she commanded. Go to the garage or the kitchen or the w. c. or the front lawn or go drown yourselves in the ocean. I don't give a damn where you go, just so you get out of here.

The group, aware that Adora, offended, was capable of cutting names off her invitation list, heeded the warning and slunk towards the door. As Mary passed her, Adora held out her hand.

I don't mean you, dearie, she said. You stay here with me.

Two

With Olive Hamilton, who worked as a responsible secretary-stenographer for a white lawyer on Wall Street—Olive herself was seven-eighths white—Mary occupied an apartment on the sixth storey of a building on Edgecombe Avenue, that pleasant thoroughfare facing the rocky cliff surmounted by City College. Neither of the girls earned very much money, but their salaries were supplemented by occasional welcome cheques from their families which made it possible for them to live comfortably, especially as Olive was an excellent cook. Mary could fry an egg and boil coffee, but here her culinary capacities ended.

Each of the girls had her own bedroom; the use of the sitting-room they shared. The sitting-room, though small, was pleasant. The furniture included an upholstered couch, several easy chairs, a desk, a table with an electric lamp, and a phonograph. Blue-flowered chintz curtains hung at the window. The walls were brightened by framed reproductions of paintings by Bellini and Carpaccio which Mary had collected during a journey through Italy.

Olive's personal taste inclined to the luxurious. Her dressing-table was hung in lace over pink satin and her bed was covered with a spread of the same materials. On the dressing-table was laid out a toilet-set of carved ivory, an extravagance which had cost her a great deal of economy in other directions. A bottle of Narcisse Noir stood near the toilet-set. Framed, on a table, and on the walls, were many photographs of friends. A French worsted doll lay dejected in one corner.

Mary's taste was more sober. There was only one picture in her room, a reproduction of the Monna Lisa. Her bed-cover was plain white; her dressing-table austere and generally devoid of articles, save for inexpensive brush, comb, and mirror. On the shelves of a bookcase were ranged volumes by James Branch Cabell, Anatole France, Jean Cocteau, Louis Bromfield, Aldous Huxley, Sherwood Anderson, Somerset Maugham, Edmond Gosse, Elinor Wylie, James Huneker, and others. Several Negro writers were represented by inscribed copies: Charles W. Chesnutt by The Conjure Woman, James Weldon Johnson by Fifty Years, Jean Toomer by Cane, Claude McKay by Harlem Shadows, W. E. B. Du Bois by The Souls of Black Folk, Walter White by The Fire in the Flint, Jessie Fauset by There is Confusion. In addition, on her writing-table stood a photograph of her father, in a silver frame, and usually a row of a dozen or so of the latest books which she had borne home from the library in an effort to keep abreast with the best of the modern output, an altruistic endeavour which enabled her to offer her patrons advice when they were in doubt, as so often she found they were.

Mary's life was simple but full: she found she had very little time to spare. Six days a week, and one evening, she worked in the library. Leaving the library usually in the afternoon around five, she often went to the Park for a walk. Then she came home, changed her dress, and read or mended her clothes while Olive cooked dinner. In the evening, frequently there would be callers: the girls knew all the young men and women in the Harlem literary circles, most of the young school-teachers, doctors, lawyers, and dentists. To some extent they mingled with, but did not entertain, the richer social set that lived in the splendid row of houses Stanford White had designed on One hundred and thirty-ninth Street, or in other pleasant localities. These people occasionally invited Mary or Olive to large dinner- or bridge-parties. The girls also encountered them at dances. It had become, Olive observed cynically to Mary, quite the thing for these more affluent folk to take up with the young intellectuals since their work had begun to appear in the Atlantic Monthly, Vanity Fair, the American Mercury, and the New Republic. The young intellectuals accepted these hitherto unfamiliar attentions without undue humility, at the same time laughing a good deal about them among themselves. Times had changed indeed when brains, rather than money, a lighter colour, or straight hair, was the password to social favour. The limits of the Blue Vein Circle were being extended.

The girls took in most of the good plays and musical entertainments, revues and song recitals alike, downtown, usually sitting in the balcony to save expense, although Olive was light enough and Mary's features were sufficiently Latin so that they were not rudely received when they asked at the box-office for places in the orchestra. Once or twice, however, when they had been escorted to the theatre by some man of darker colour, they had been caused some humiliation and embarrassment. On one such occasion, after the usher had seated them, the house-manager had descended the aisle to demand a view of their stubs. On examination, he informed them that a mistake had been made, assuring them that their seats were for another night. He refused, moreover, to relinquish the stubs and escorted them to the lobby where he stated that he would willingly exchange them for balcony tickets, as the orchestra for this particular evening had been sold out. The lesson was learned. Thereafter Olive always took charge of the stubs and, if a view of them were requested, held them up so that the figures might be deciphered, but refused to permit them to leave her fingers.

Occasionally, caught in the lower part of town at an inconvenient hour, the question arose as to where one might eat. Olive alone was white enough to be spared any anxiety on this count, and even Mary, accompanied by Olive, succeeded in passing, but when their companion had unmistakably African features, difficulties arose. Once, indeed, when their escort had been a very black Negro of international reputation they had been ejected from a hotel dining-room. The head-waiter who was acquainted with Olive and was quite aware that she had Negro blood, explained that he himself had no objection to serving coloured people, but that X—— was so undeniably black that the patrons of the restaurant might object to his proximity. The taboo, it appeared, was solely one of colour, and there were, it sometimes occurred to Mary, the highest advantages, both social and economic, in being near white or yellow, or, if dark, possessed of Spanish features and glib enough with words in some foreign tongue to convince the waiter that one belonged to a dark European race, but, unfortunately, as Olive knew well to her cost—she had once been insulted by a policeman because a black man had accompanied her to a Negro restaurant—in certain public places in Harlem the reverse difficulty arose.

With one young man in particular, Howard Allison, the girls were accustomed to discuss these and allied problems which touched their very existence. Allison's father had been born a slave. He was nine years old when he was freed. Later he had become an itinerant preacher. By scrimping, his family had managed to send Howard to Harvard, and afterwards to Columbia Law School. He had just begun to practise his profession; as yet he was quite destitute of clients. Handsome and tall, dark brown in colour, he had personal reasons for being seriously interested in the perplexing phases of the Negro problem.

One night he came in after dinner—Olive, expecting him, had prepared a large pot of coffee—with Richard Fort Sill, a young man who was so white that, like Olive, below the line he was never taken for a Negro.

They became expansive over the coffee and cigarettes.

Of course, Howard was saying, it isn't so bad for us as it was for those who came before. We at least have Harlem.

Sill began to snicker. The Mecca of the New Negro! The City of Refuge! he cried derisively.

I don't know that we even have Harlem, Olive argued, so many white people come up here now to the cabarets. Why, in one or two places they've actually tried to do a little jim crowing!

Think of it! Howard replied. It isn't, he went on, that we want to mingle with the whites—I mean that we don't want to much more than we are already compelled to—but it is a bore to have them all over our places while we are excluded from their theatres and restaurants merely on account of our colour, theatres and restaurants which admit Chinese and Hindus—if I wore a turban or a burnous I could go anywhere—and prostitutes of any nationality. Why, a white prostitute can go places where a coloured preacher would be refused admittance.

True enough, Counsellor, Sill drawled. There's no social line drawn in jail anyway. Probably Marcus Garvey is treated just as well as his fellow convicts. . . . He was lounging in a chair with his hand hanging so far over one arm that his cigarette almost singed the rug. . . . It all comes down, he went on, to that question the ofays are always asking each other: would you like your sister to marry a Negro? You must realize, my dear coloured brethren, that social equality means a mingling of the sexes of the two races. Sill's tone was tinged with a bitter irony.

Well, Howard laughed, the buckras should have thought of that earlier, before you were born, Dick. How did you get as white as you are?

The Southern explanation is that Sherman marched to the sea.

They all laughed.

He must have had a considerable and very vital army, was Olive's comment. You know as well as I do that practically every other ofay in the South has a coloured half-brother and you know how many successful intermarriages there have been, especially in the West Indies. It strikes me as particularly amusing what they have to say, these ofays, about the geniuses of our race. Oh yes, they admit that

Pushkin was a genius, that Dumas was a genius, but it was because they had white blood! Apparently miscegenation is a very fine thing indeed after it has happened, but for God's sake don't let it happen!

You know very well, Mary inserted, as she set down her empty cup, that the best people of *our* race object to mixed marriages more strenuously than the whites do. I believe if the social barriers were let down there would be fewer of them than there are now.

And if the barriers were let down, another great factor would be eliminated, Howard asserted, the present advantage of being as near white as possible. Why, the white Negro—you, Dick, or Olive—can go anywhere, to any hotel or theatre, without being challenged. You know the number of us that have gone even farther than that.

Buda Green is passing, Olive put in. I met her on Fifth Avenue last Sunday. She was with a white man and she tipped me a wink. Later, she called me up and told me all about it. You can't blame her. I couldn't do it, though. No matter what happens, I stick to my race.

Mary noted that a more intense expression had come into Dick Sill's face.

You say that, he said, but I wonder how much you mean. Think how much easier it is to get jobs if you don't acknowledge your race. Why, even in the Negro theatre they won't engage dark girls. In *their* world, the white world, they won't even give you a look-in at anything good if you're not somewhere near their colour. Ollie, do you think for one moment you'd be engaged as a private secretary if you were black? You know you wouldn't. And the same thing is true of me. Well, I've thought it all out and I'm going to pass!

Dick! The trio cried out simultaneously.

Yes, he went on defiantly. Not today or tomorrow perhaps, but sooner or later I'm going to pass, go over the line, and marry a white woman. It serves them jolly well right for forcing us to. I'd like to start a movement for all us near whites to pass. In a short time there wouldn't be any Negro problem. There wouldn't even be any Negroes.

Well, a good many have preceded you, Howard said. I've heard there are about eight thousand in New York alone.

I couldn't do it, Olive asserted. I just couldn't do it. Somehow I feel my race.

What race? cried Dick. What race do you feel? If you lived in Brazil and had one drop of white blood you'd be considered white. Here the reverse is true. What's the coloured race ever done for you? Dick, now thoroughly worked up, demanded. What?

Well, they haven't done anything particularly for or against me, but somehow in spirit I belong to them. I know that. I don't *feel* white. What you do is your business, just as it's Buda's business. I just couldn't do it myself, that's all.

Mary was conciliatory. We go round and round like squirrels in a cage and we never get anywhere, she said. Is there any solution? Sometimes I like to think there is, and sometimes I don't really care. Do you know, when we keep away from this subject, we have so much pleasure among ourselves that I sometimes think it isn't very important . . . she hesitated . . . if a thoughtless white person occasionally is rude. You can laugh all you like, Dick, but Harlem *is* a sort of Mecca. In some ways it's even an advantage to be coloured. Certainly on the stage it's no handicap. It's almost an asset. And now the white editors are beginning to regard Negroes as interesting novelties, like white elephants or black roses. They'll print practically anything our coloured writers send in. . . .

That won't last. Dick interrupted her fiercely. The time is coming and soon enough, at that, when the Negro artist will have to compete with the white artist on an equal plane if he expects to make any impression. I think the ofays must be getting tired of saying "Pretty good for a Nigger."

Howard had been meditating. I believe, he said at last, a trifle sententiously, Mary thought, that there is a solution for what is called the race problem. . . . The others all stared at him. . . . You know old Booker T was all for conciliation; then Du Bois came along and was all for an aggressive policy. Now neither of these methods worked for a very simple reason, because fundamentally, and generally speaking, the white race is not vitally interested in the Negro problem. In the mass they are quite indifferent to it. It doesn't bother *them,* so they just forget it. I learned that much at Harvard. They don't argue about it or even think about it much. Rather, they are inclined to ignore it, until some jig or other annoys them and then they lynch him or start a riot or something.

Then, he continued, still speaking earnestly, there is the policy of the young coloured intellectuals, from whom we have heard so much during the past two years, which is simply to adopt a mental attitude of equality and break the bars down gradually through the work of our artists. That won't be successful either, except for the artists. Of course, Paul Robeson and Roland Hayes and Countée Cullen can go anywhere within reason. They will be invited to white dinner parties, but I don't see how that's going to affect the rest of us.

Why not? Olive demanded.

Because the white people they meet will regard them as geniuses, in other words, exceptions. Yes, they will say to themselves, these are certainly unusually brilliant and delightful individuals; it's a pity all Negroes aren't like them. So they will go on neglecting the plight in which our respectable middle class finds itself.

Well, Mary said, I thought you had a solution.

So I have. It's simple enough to state, not so

easy to achieve. It's merely economic. As soon as we, in the mass, become rich enough we will become powerful. You can't keep up the bars when your pocket-book is affected, no matter how violent your prejudice. As soon as we are rich enough, we will go wherever we really want to go, and do what we want to do. White people may sneer at us, but they will receive us. Look at the Jews. A lot of Nordics despise them, but they can't ignore them. They're much too important financially.

But, Counsellor, you're only stating Booker T's old premise, Dick put in. He said all that—not, to be sure, quite so bluntly—and what has happened? Any time one of us saves a little money, the white world becomes green-eyed with jealousy, to say nothing of our own group.

Booker T did say something like that tentatively, Howard admitted, but we've got to work faster than he expected us to. He urged Negroes to acquire land and work it. It's better to acquire land and sell it. And it's true that in the South the poor whites are envious if we get on and in Harlem the shines are jealous. I said it was going to be difficult. All of us have very serious handicaps to overcome. Nevertheless . . .

Bottle it, Howard, Olive cried, yawning. I've heard enough of this lecture for one evening. Let's listen to Clara Smith. She wound up the phonograph and put on a record. Soon the moaning wonder of the Blues singer's voice sounded in the little room:

Ah wants to hop a train an'
Go where duh town is clean.
Wants to hop a train, Lawd!
Go where duh town is clean,
Folks roun' heah is so low-down an' mean.

The tears were streaming down Mary's cheeks. The others were sitting in solemn, dejected silence.

Oh hell, Ollie, Dick complained, I don't see that you've improved matters much. Try the Funny Blues!

Three

Four or five weeks had slipped by almost imperceptibly since the week-end party at Adora's when one day, taking stock, Mary was amazed to discover that, although she had written her mother at least once every week, she had not mentioned the proposal made her by Randolph Pettijohn. Proposals of marriage were rare enough, eventful enough, so that they deserved at least a passing reference in the chronicle of events she sent home, more especially because, till now, her mother had enjoyed what practically amounted to her complete confidence. As a matter of self-discipline and to discover the truth in her own soul, if such a thing were possible, Mary sat down to her desk to repair the omission and tried faithfully to give a true account of what had occurred, with her own reaction to it. After she had penned the last line she realized why she hadn't written about this particular incident before: she had been ashamed. Ashamed to confess to her mother that she had attracted the attention of such a man. She was also, almost mystically, aware of something else: Byron Kasson had enlisted her sympathy, awakened her imagination, to an extraordinary degree. Olive had often assured Mary that she was cold. Everybody says you're cold, that you have no natural feeling, Olive had complained. Why don't you let yourself go once in a while? There was at least this much truth in this criticism, Mary confessed to herself, that she did not let herself go. She had an instinctive horror of promiscuity, of being handled, even touched, by a man who did not mean a good deal to her. This might, she sometimes argued with herself, have something to do with her white inheritance, but Olive, who was far whiter, was lacking in this inherent sense of prudery. At any rate, whatever the cause, Mary realized that she was different in this respect from most of the other girls she knew. The Negro blood was there, warm and passionately earnest: all her preferences and prejudices were on the side of the race into which she had been born. She was as capable, she was convinced, of amorous emotion, as any of her friends, but the fact remained that she was more selective. Oh, the others were respectable enough; they did not involve themselves too deeply. On the other hand, they did not flee from a kiss in the dark. A casual kiss in the dark was a repellant idea to Mary. What she wanted was a kiss in the light—with the right man, and the right man hitherto had never appeared. Now, thinking of Byron Kasson, she trembled as she gradually became aware of what sort of acknowledgment she was dragging out of her innermost soul. It startled her somewhat to perceive how little unwelcome to her it would be to encounter this man again. She did not mention Byron Kasson in her letter to her mother nor, conscious of this fact, could she bring herself to do so.

It was the middle of September; the sky was overcast with clouds and a slight drizzle was falling. Ollie had not yet returned from the office. Mary, alone, decided that a walk would agree admirably with her mood. Slipping a blue jersey and a raincoat over her woollen frock and pulling a tam-o'-shanter over her head, she started forth. The wind had risen and the raindrops increased in size. They beat against her cheeks and wet her hair and ankles. Tingling with health, she was grateful for this attention from the elements.

It had been, she reflected, a pleasant week. She had principally been occupied in borrowing from several private collections specimens of primitive African sculpture and she had been astonishingly successful—lucky, she called it—in unearthing worthy examples, representing the creative skill of a variety of tribes from different localities in Africa. Moreover, early dates were more or less reasonably ascribed to some of them. One strangely beautiful head was said to have been executed in the tenth century, or even earlier, while a box, exquisite in proportion and design, was said to have been created in the fourteenth century. Mary was beginning to recognize the feel of the older work, the soft, smooth texture, like that of the best Chinese porcelains, of the wood, so different from that of the coarser, later pieces. She knew something too, now, about the more primitive design, lovelier in its conception, because it was more honest, than the more elaborate, later traceries, created under Portuguese influence. . . . There had been a pleasant dinner party or two; she recalled with particular pleasure an evening at the Weston Underwoods' when she had met the new secretary to the Haytian consul. He spoke only French and she welcomed this opportunity to practise the language with a young man made more tolerant, perhaps, by his obvious interest in herself. It was agreeable, too, to meet some one who knew a great deal about Cocteau and Morand and Proust, knew about them, that is, in their relation to French literature in general. René Maran, the author of Batouala, he had actually been acquainted with. . . . One night, with Howard and Olive, she had witnessed Arms and the Man at the Guild Theatre, and another she had attended a rent-party, given by some indigent girl friends, had paid fifty cents, and had been rewarded by a shower of gin and orange-juice over the front of one of her favourite frocks. Carbona, the next morning, had only partially removed the stain. The clumsy young man who had been responsible for the catastrophe had seemed more put out by the loss of the gin—his carelessness had exhausted the supply—than over the injury to her dress. Otherwise, however, it had been a gay evening. There had been dancing to the music of a phonograph in a two-room apartment

—the dimensions of the largest chamber were about twelve by eight feet—and she had danced until two. Nearly everybody danced every night: why? Mary asked herself. Is it that we want to forget? She was reminded of a Negro story called Melanctha, in Gertrude Stein's Three Lives. A white assistant in the library had brought this book to her to read and she had been recommending it ever since, but it seemed that no other copies were available. She recalled now a passage from this story which she had committed to memory. Dr. Campbell was speaking to Melanctha: It ain't very easy for you to understand what I was meaning by what I was just saying to you, and perhaps some of the good people I like so wouldn't think very much, any more than you do, Miss Melanctha, about the ways I have to be good. But that's no matter Miss Melanctha. What I mean Miss Melanctha by what I was just saying to you is, that I don't, no, never, believe in doing things just to get excited. You see Miss Melanctha I mean the way so many of the coloured people do it. Instead of just working hard and caring about their working and living regular with their families and saving up all their money, so they will have some to bring their children up better, instead of living regular and doing like that and getting all their new ways from just decent living, the coloured people just keep running around and perhaps drinking and doing everything bad they can ever think of, and not just because they like all those bad things that they are always doing, but only just because they want to get excited. No, Miss Melanctha, you see I am a coloured man myself and I ain't sorry, and I want to see the coloured people being good and careful and always honest and living just as regular as can be, and I am sure Miss Melanctha, that that way everybody can have a good time, and be happy and keep right and be busy, and not always have to be doing bad things for new ways to get excited. Yes, Miss Melanctha, I certainly do like everything to be good, and quiet, and I certainly do think that is the best way for all us coloured people. No, Miss Melanctha too, I don't mean this except only just the way I say it. I ain't got any other meaning Miss Melanctha, and it's that what I mean when I am saying about being really good. It ain't Miss Melanctha to be pious and not liking every kind of people, and I don't say ever Miss Melanctha that when other kind of people come regular into your life you shouldn't want to know them always. What I mean Miss Melanctha by what I am always saying is, you shouldn't try to know everybody just to run around and get excited. It's that kind of way of doing that I hate so always Miss Melanctha, and that is so bad for all us coloured people. I don't know as you understand now any better what I mean by what I was just saying to you. But you certainly do know now Miss Melanctha, that I always mean it what I say when I am talking. . . . Some time during the evening a strange young man with a deep baritone voice —the quality reminded her a little of Paul Robeson's —and a simple faith had sung Spirituals. Mary, recalling, softly murmured:

> Oh, gi' me yo' han', gi' me yo' han';
> All Ah want is duh love o' God;
> Gi' me yo' han', gi' me yo' han';
> You mus' be lovin' at God's comman'.
>
> You say duh Lord has set you free,
> You mus' be lovin' at God's comman',
> Why doan you let yo' neighbour be,
> You mus' be lovin' at . . .

Funny thing about the Spirituals, Mary reflected. I'm not religious. Nobody I know is really religious. We are, for the most part, pagans, natural pagans, but when we were slaves we turned naturally and gratefully to a religion which promised joy everlasting and a reunion with relatives—sold up and down the river—in the life to come. Now, when oppression has been removed from some of us, we revert quite simply to paganism. Those from whom it has not been removed—the servant-girls and the poor—are glad to continue to pray and shout, but I don't believe they really feel faith—except as an escape from the drudgery of their lives. They don't really stop playing Numbers or dancing on Sunday or anything else that their religion forbids them to do. They enjoy themselves in church on Sunday as they do in the cabarets on week-days. But the people who created the Spirituals must have felt a real faith, and that is why, I suppose, they touch most of us, knock us off our pins, and make us want to cry or shout.

Mary had arrived at the Park without encountering an acquaintance. She struck out down a path, the wet gravel crunching under her boots, the raindrops tossed by the wind from the dying leaves whipping her cheeks. She passed a clearing where a few days before, she remembered, she had witnessed a strange ceremony: some black people from one of the British West Indies—monkey-chasers they called them on Lenox Avenue; what a good story Rudolph Fisher had woven about one of them and the general Harlem attitude of distrust and even active dislike which they awakened—playing cricket with proper bats and wickets. She had stood for a moment watching them and listening to their Cockney speech. What a people we are! she meditated, cast into alien lands all over the earth, conforming, whether we like it or not, to the customs and manners and laws of folk who despise us, and yet everywhere, in spite of all obstacles, we manage to keep something of our own, even to make something of it. What other race in America, or anywhere else for that matter, has produced anything better than the Spirituals? Anything as good? was her succeeding interrogative boast. Yet the Spirituals had sprung from ignorant slaves, bending under the lash. Unknown black bards, James Weldon Johnson had beautifully called them. . . .

On her return to the apartment she discovered Olive on her knees in the kitchen mopping up a lake of cream.

Why is it, Olive demanded with a groan, that one can never open an ice-box door without something popping out?

Can I help you, Ollie?

Well, Mary, I wish you'd look at my holy bran muffins in the oven and see if they are done.

After complying with Olive's request, Mary went to her room, removed her wet clothes, washed and towelled herself thoroughly, drew on a dressing-gown and was ready for dinner.

Immediately they sat down to table, Olive began to chatter.

I stopped in at George Lister's this afternoon to make an appointment. Believe me, that sheik is popular. I don't know whether it's because he's such a good dentist or whether it's just his looks. The waiting-room was crowded. It was like a Sunday morning service at Abyssinian Baptist.

How's Lenore?

Oh, George says she's doing all right and of course he assured me the baby is sweet.

We ought to go to see Lenore.

Um. Olive's mouth was full of fried chicken. After a little she went on, Howard's got a case.

No! I'm so glad, Ollie!

Yes, he's defending a poor old grandpa who is victim of a landlord. He's going to invoke the rent laws. Naturally, she added, he won't get a cent.

Poor Howard! He's had such a time getting started.

I don't mean maybe! He's got guts, though. Sometimes I wonder how he can stick it out.

They all have to begin. Doctors and lawyers can't advertise: it isn't considered professional.

I know, but look at George's practice.

Well, there aren't so many good dentists.

Not so many good-looking ones, at any rate.

They ate in silence for a time.

Where did you hear about Howard? Mary inquired.

He telephoned me. . . . Mary was aware of a curious clang-tint in Olive's voice. . . . Saw Sergia Sawyer at George's.

You must have picked up a lot of gossip.

She talked as fast as her tongue would wag. Said Buda Green's going to marry that Mr. Eddie.

He doesn't know?

And nobody's going to tell him. It's funny, Olive went on, as she poured the rich chicken gravy over her mashed potatoes, how we love to fool white people.

Of course, she said, you can understand those cotton-picking jigs in the South; they've had to put up with centuries of deceit and treachery on the part of the ofays, but we—people like you and me—are that way too. We've never suffered from white deceit and treachery and yet we're more or less like the others when it comes to handing the bunk to the ofays. Whenever my boss asks me a question and the correct answer would be derogatory to my race, I just naturally lie to him, although he's honestly interested. I can't help it. We're all alike that way.

A broad smile spread over Olive's face.

What are you laughing about, Ollie? Mary demanded.

I was thinking of a funny story the boss told me about his coloured butler. It seems Sam was several hours late one day and he apologized for his tardiness by explaining there had been a fire. The boss was solicitous. Did you lose much? he asked him. Everything Ah had, said Sam; Duh house burn 'way down to duh groun'; not a brick lef'. A day or two later the boss asks Sam what his new address is, and Sam replies: Why, Ah's livin' at duh same place.

Mary laughed as she spread butter on a bran muffin.

What else did Sergia tell you? she inquired.

Olive opened her eyes. Well, I'm glad to see you falling for gossip, Mary. That's hopefully human. Next you'll be falling for a pair of Oxford bags.

Don't tease me, Ollie.

I'm not teasing you, but I wish you'd be a little more open to infection. You must have been vaccinated against love. . . . I think, she added with some embarrassment, I'm going to marry Howard. . . . She made this announcement in a manner which suggested that the idea had just occurred to her.

Ollie dear, I'm so glad. Mary rose from her place to kiss her friend. When was it settled?

I told him last night that I thought I would and today I know I will. It's going to be soon, too. I'm not going to put it off till he's a regular butter and egg man. What's the use of waiting?

I'll miss you, Ollie.

I'll miss you too, you old darling. Olive impulsively ran around the table to return her friend's embrace. But we'll see a lot of each other just the same.

Mary went to the kitchen to bring in the blue Canton china dessert plates heaped with an aromatic pudding.

Sergia says Lasca Sartoris is back from Paris, Olive remarked.

Lasca the legendary! Where is she stopping?

With Sylvia for a few weeks until she can find an apartment. Sergia says she's brought back a flock of trunks: Poiret and Vionnet gowns and Reboux hats and fans and shoes and shawls and perfumes enough to fit out the whole Follies cast.

After she had assisted Olive in clearing the table and washing the dishes, Mary retired to her room to dress. Olive was waiting for Howard. Mary had promised to attend a party at Hester Albright's, a prospect which aroused in her no anticipations of pleasure. Hester, a spinster of thirty-eight, lived with her mother, a deaf, querulous, garrulous, tiresome, old lady, on the fourth floor of an apartment building on St. Nicholas Avenue. They had migrated from Washington to Harlem about five years previously. Why, nobody exactly understood, as Washington society, according to Hester, was immeasurably superior to the Harlem variety. She was in the habit, indeed, of making invidious comparisons, the more mysterious when one considered that the Albrights apparently were sufficiently well off to live comfortably wherever they might choose. As a matter of fact, living expenses in Harlem were higher than in the national capital. I think, Olive had once remarked, that it amuses them to live here so they can tell us how awful we are. . . . If Hester and her mother looked down on Harlem, they did not enjoy a similar privilege with Brooklyn. The Brooklyn set ignored their very existence.

Hester was plain, far too plain to receive masculine attentions, but vain enough to conceive herself as irresistible. A thorough prig, she was easily shocked. She was, moreover, extremely critical, not only of others' actions but also of their very thoughts. She cherished her own idiosyncratic ideas about propriety, propriety in art, in dressing, in general conduct. She particularly assumed an aggressive and antagonistic attitude towards the new literary group which was springing up in Harlem, albeit it was fostered by most of the older intellectuals as one of the most promising indications of an eventual Negro supremacy. This antagonism, Mary suspected, was inspired by the fact that this younger group was more inclined to write about the squalor and vice of Harlem life than about the respectable elegance of Washington society.

About twice a year, moved, doubtless, Mary conceived, by some vaguely charitable urge—I must be kind to this poor girl, Mary could imagine her as thinking—Hester invited Mary to her home and Mary, who considered it her duty as a librarian to mingle with as many different kinds of people as possible, dutifully accepted these invitations.

Tonight, however, she assured herself ruefully, as she surveyed her reflection and smoothed out her pale-blue silk dress before the mirror, she was in no mood for this expedition. Olive's announcement, coming as it had fast on her own self-admission in the afternoon, had somewhat upset her. She would have preferred remaining at home with Howard and Olive, later retiring to her own room where she might give herself up to her thoughts and make some attempt to unravel her perplexing mental tangle. She reminded herself, however, that she had given her promise, and she invariably made it a rigid rule of conduct to keep engagements to which she had pledged herself. Nevertheless a sigh escaped her as she raised the shade to open the window. It was no longer raining, she perceived, and she could therefore easily walk the short distance to the Albrights' apartment.

It was shortly after nine when Hester opened the door for her—the Albrights did not keep a servant.

Rest your wrap, Mary, Hester adjured her and then led her guest into the tiny sitting-room where Mrs. Albright, a withered, wrinkled, old woman with a hooked nose, waved her ear-trumpet sceptre from her arm-chair throne. On the other side of the cheerful, open fire sat Orville Snodes, who was something or other at the Harlem Y. M. C. A. Mary detested him, with no more personal reason for doing so than the fact that he bored her. The mere sight of his round, brown, empty face, so like an Ethiopian moon, exasperated her.

How are you, Mrs. Albright? Mary greeted the old lady.

How have you been? Hester's ancient mother croaked.

Mary let her relaxed palm fall limply into Orville Snodes's hand.

Mrs. Albright was the widow of a building-contractor and it had always been understood—although no one had ever heard Mrs. Albright say so directly—that she felt she had married beneath her, despite the fact that she owed her present easy mode of living to this curious expression of humility. At any rate, whatever might be her state of mind in regard to this episode, she had made at least one concession to convention by permitting the photograph of her late sire to remain in plain view on the mantelpiece. He had a pleasant face, Mary thought, when she regarded it, as she frequently did, in an attempt to decipher an excuse for the mating of this alien pair. His huge, white moustaches, decorating the centre of his honest, black countenance, gave him rather the appearance of a friendly walrus, and a deep scar, almost white, extending from the left corner of his lip to his left eye, added a human touch. It was obvious, Mary thought, that some time or other he had been cut by an inimical razor. How Mrs. Albright must have shuddered at this squalid indignity!

This evening the old lady appeared to be in a most benign mood. The fire, at least temporarily, had thawed out her cold spirit. At any rate, this was Mary's initial impression, as she observed Mrs. Albright nodding her head back and forward with a slow, languid movement, lazily drinking in the warmth.

I have asked a very few tonight, a very few, Hester was explaining. I like small parties better. They are so much more intime.

Oh, beaucoup, beaucoup plus, corroborated Orville. Man wants but little here below, nor wants that little long, he quoted. Then, so unexpectedly that Mary had a feeling that he was almost challenging her to reply affirmatively, he demanded:

Have you been to the Metropolitan Art Museum lately?

No, she managed to stutter, with a distinct sensation of guilt.

The pictures are very beautiful, très, très, beaux, Orville announced, rubbing his tiny hands together. His round, brown face and his bald head appeared to glow with his enthusiasm. J'aime beaucoup l'art, he added.

What's that? Mrs. Albright screamed, lifting her trumpet still higher. What did Orville say, Hester?

He says he just loves art, mama.

So do I. . . . The old lady positively beamed. . . . I've always loved art, even as a girl. In Washington, where I come from, people—that is, people that we know—have pictures in their houses, paintings. Do you remember the Willetts' house, Hester?

Why, of course I do, mama! What a question! Our dear friends, the Willetts, she explained to her guests. Such elegance! Such taste!

Well, the Willetts have an art gallery, Mary, Mrs. Albright continued, a beautiful, long gallery with paintings in oil of trees and birds. No nudes. Nothing disgusting. It is all charming and respectable. I do not believe I know any one here who has any good pictures. New York is very different from Washington, she sighed.

Now take that picture over there. Hester pointed to a canvas on which were depicted a waterfall, a ruined castle, and a rustic bridge on which trudged a milkmaid bearing a pail. It was perhaps the tenth occasion on which Mary had been invited to regard it appreciatively. That picture, Hester went on, was presented to papa by a gentleman for whom he had built a house. It is, she added impressively, a Ridgeway Knight.

Très, très beau, Orville pronounced. I have always admired it.

Very pretty, Mary managed to stammer. If you are so much interested in art, perhaps I can persuade you to visit my exhibition of African sculpture.

What's that? Mrs. Albright demanded.

An exhibition at the library, mother. Hester turned to Mary: African sculpture! That dreadful, vulgar stuff!

I think it's very wonderful, said Mary, perhaps a little warmly.

You don't have to yell at me. I can hear you, Mrs. Albright shrieked almost savagely. Like most deaf persons she hated to have visitors raise their voices.

It's the work of heathen savages, Hester protested hotly, and it has nothing to do with art.

Sauvages! translated Orville emphatically. Sauvages!

Tney were our ancestors, Mary asserted.

Of course, Hester replied, everybody goes back to savages, but it does no good to unearth that sort of thing. Why, I saw one of the creatures once and I was ashamed. Horrible, woolly-headed barbarian! He was positively indecent. She shuddered.

Obscene: Orville offered the room a synonym.

What's that? the old lady demanded. Nobody seems to care whether I hear or not, she whimpered.

African statues are obscene, mama, cried Hester.

Seen? Seen where? inquired the deaf woman, staring about her with great vigour.

Not respectable, screamed her daughter.

Who's not respectable?

African wood-carving.

I should think not! I should think not indeed, Mrs. Albright proclaimed, adding with great indignation, Certainly not. In Wash . . .

There was a welcome interruption. In answer to the bell, Hester admitted Conrad Gladbrook, a shy, young school-teacher, and his wife. Mary knew them only slightly. Mrs. Gladbrook was a very black, very short woman who had a nervous habit of throwing her head back and giggling, exposing two rows of fine white teeth, and who seemed incapable of emitting an intelligent syllable. Almost immediately after the arrival of the Gladbrooks, Mary was happy to hear Webb Leverett's voice at the door. He, at least, could sing.

Oh, Webb, I'm so glad you've come, Hester

greeted him. Rest your coat, please. Now we can have some music.

Isn't it a little early for music? Webb protested.

Of course, I'll give you some coffee first.

While Hester was out of the room, every one sat about in more or less open discomfort, that is every one but Mrs. Albright. Now and again, for no apparent reason, Mrs. Gladbrook tossed back her head and giggled. Fortunately, she was sitting behind Mrs. Albright who, at intervals, muttered with great ferocity, Certainly not! Presently Hester returned with a tray on which was set out a Sheffield service, very old and lovely, Mary thought, flanked by delicate porcelain cups.

You pour, mama, Hester suggested.

Is it still raining? Orville inquired of the latecomers.

I think it has stopped, Conrad Gladbrook replied.

His wife giggled nervously.

It's stopped raining, mama, Hester announced.

I never said it hadn't, her mother replied testily. Will you take cream, Mrs. Gladbrook?

Please, that lady barely whispered.

I asked you if you take cream? Mrs. Albright thundered.

She says she'll have some, mama.

I say: Webb was addressing Mary, I've been to see your exhibition. It's too wonderful!

Mary thanked him, but did not pursue the subject. It seemed to her that she had heard enough about this exhibition for one evening. Have you, she demanded, as she stirred her coffee, read John Bolivar's new story?

Hester, who was passing sandwiches, replied to this question which had not been addressed to her. Oh, she averred, I have. What a vulgar story! How can he write about such vulgar people? Why, even here in Harlem there are plenty of doctors and lawyers and in Washington we have a real society. I don't see any use of dragging up all that muck. Nobody wants to read about *that.*

I quite agree with you, Orville said. Quite. Honi soit qui mal y pense.

Mary smiled in spite of herself. Perhaps, she urged, in a mild attempt to defend the absent author, the milieu he describes is more novel and picturesque than that which surrounds the life of a physician or a lawyer.

Why, Mary, how can you say such a thing? Hester demanded. I think it is shameless.

Mary was desperate. Won't you sing, Webb? she pleaded.

Oh, oui. Chantez, s'il vous plaît, chantez! piped Orville.

Webb sings so well, Hester informed the bashful Gladbrooks. Mrs. Gladbrook giggled.

Fetching his music roll from the hall, Webb went to the upright piano. There, after considerable fumbling, he selected a piece of music, and began to sing, playing his own accompaniment:

Hark! hark the lark at heaven's gate sings,
   And Phœbus 'gins arise,
His steeds to water at those springs
   On chaliced flowers that lies;
And winking Mary-buds begin
   To ope their golden eyes:
With every thing that pretty is.
   My lady sweet, arise;
      Arise, arise!

Webb sang in rather an uncertain tenor voice. His tones often stuck in his throat. He did not know very well how to control them, Mary noted. The others sat up very stiffly while he sang, and when he had concluded, Hester remarked, Delightful!

This sentiment was feebly echoed by her guests.

Sing another, Hester suggested. Can you hear, mama?

Perfectly.

Webb pawed about among his music again and eventually dragged out another song.

Who is Sylvia? what is she?
   That all our swains commend her:
Holy, fair, and wise is she;
   The heaven such grace did lend her,
That she might admired be.
Is she kind, as she is fair?
   For beauty lives with kindness:
Love doth to her eyes repair,
   To help him of his blindness.

Very pretty, Hester pronounced, stifling a yawn.

Classic and sweet, Orville asserted. A true gem.

A mischievous spirit prompted Mary to inquire, Do you know any Spirituals?

One or two, Webb admitted.

Oh, do sing one, please.

Webb faced the room, standing. Hester's face was iron.

I sing Spirituals without accompaniment, he explained, and then began very simply:

Walk together, children,
Don't you get weary,
Walk together, children,
Don't you get weary,
There's a great Camp-meeting in the Promised Land.

Going to mourn and never tire
Mourn and never tire,
Mourn and never tire,
There's a great Camp-meeting in the Promised Land.

Mary noted at once how the feeling in this music dominated him, transfigured his voice, caused one to forget the serious faults of his singing. Even without the dialect, the song sounded sincere. And the room! What a change! Mrs. Gladbrook was crying. Gladbrook and Orville were swaying to the rhythm while Mrs. Albright moved her ear-trumpet, as though it were a baton, up and down to the beat.

After a short silence, Webb spontaneously began a livelier number:

Ezekiel saw the wheel
'Way up in the middle of the air;
Ezekiel saw the wheel,
'Way in the middle of the air;
And the little wheel run by faith,
And the big wheel run by the grace of God;
'Tis a wheel in a wheel,
'Way in the middle of the air.

As Webb rendered this song of simple faith, Mary witnessed what seemed to be a miracle: Hester's shoulders moved from side to side to the rhythm, while her lips formed the words of the stanza.

Four

A day or so later, Mary encountered Adora emerging from a shop on Seventh Avenue.

You haven't been to see me since I came back from the country, the ex-music-hall diva complained. I've a good mind to cut you dead.

Don't scold me, Mary pleaded. You know I'm a working woman.

I know you have more time than I have, Adora retorted, but I don't care how you behave. I like you and I'm going to hang on to you. Come home with me now.

Assenting willingly, Mary entered the Rolls-Royce, whereupon the chauffeur in purple livery slammed the door and drove the pair the short distance to West One hundred and thirty-ninth Street, dubbed Strivers' Row by all and sundry in Harlem. This block of tan brick houses, flanked by rows of trees on either side of the way, had been designed in the early twentieth century by Stanford White, at the time when Harlem was a German section. Now they had been taken over by rich Negroes: a few, like Fletcher Henderson, the band-leader, and Harry Wills, the prize-fighter, of international fame, but most of them lawyers, physicians, real-estate operators, or opulent proprietors of beauty parlours. Mary remembered that she had read an editorial in Opportunity, based on advertising statistics, which seemed to prove that her race spent more money on hair-straighteners and skin-lightening preparations than they did on food or clothing. It was peculiarly ironic, Mary thought in this connection, that while the coloured women were making such an effort to have their hair uncurled, the white women were undergoing the horrors incident to the production of the permanent wave.

Adora's house stood near the centre of the block, and entrance to it, as was the case with the other dwellings on this pleasant street, was effected by ascending a few steps above the sidewalk. In the hallway the hostess paused long enough to throw aside her leather sport-coat, adjuring Mary to follow her example before she led her upstairs into the drawing-room.

Sit down a minute, Adora invited, as she disappeared up another flight of stairs.

Mary did not sit down. Instead, she seized the occasion to look around, for she had never been in this house before, and her interest in beautiful rooms was enduring. She sometimes wondered from what remote ancestor she had inherited this love of luxury which came to the fore whenever it was given a reasonable opportunity. Ordinarily, however, she succeeded in burying it in her subconsciousness, as she could not afford to indulge her own tastes. However she was not envious of others.

Indeed, she derived as much pleasure from the appraisal and admiration of beautiful objects in an art gallery as she would have, had they belonged to her.

Most of the furniture in the room was representative of the Louis XVI epoch, Mary, who had passed long hours studying period-rooms in the Metropolitan Museum of Art, recognized at once, and it pleased her to be aware that she could distinguish the chairs which had recently been upholstered from those which still preserved their original brocades. The walls were hung in a pale-lavender satin, and adorned, here and there, with pictures, Fragonard or Boucher sketches, or something very like them. On the tea-table a Sèvres service, in turquoise and amethyst paste, was laid out. The carpet was Aubusson. On the mantelpiece, between a clock and two candlesticks, also Sèvres, stood a few photographs framed in silver. One of these in particular caught and held Mary's attention.

This was a photograph of a lady in evening-dress, seated beside two Pekinese spaniels on a Victorian couch. Across the knees of the unknown, trailing carelessly over the arm of the couch, the long fringe sweeping the floor, was spread a Spanish shawl, embroidered in fantastic flowers. The lady was of a surpassing loveliness. Apparently light brown—very like my own colour, Mary decided—certainly much darker than yellow or tan, the features were not Negroid. Rather they suggested a Spanish or a Portuguese origin. The nose was delicate, the mouth provocative and sensual. Pear-shaped pearls depended from the lobes of the tiny ears. The black, wavy hair was combed severely back from the forehead, above the ears, and shingled. The lady was dressed in the smartest mode of the moment; moreover, Mary observed at once, she wore her clothes with that manner which is rare with women of any race or colour. During the comparatively short period she had lived in Harlem, Mary had been a constant attendant at the white theatres in New York; she frequently had an opportunity to study white women in restaurants; with a few she even was personally acquainted. The beauties of Harlem were all known to her; she recognized at sight the more celebrated dancers and singers engaged in vaudeville or the coloured revues. She could not, however, at the moment, bring to mind a single figure of either race—she excepted, on reflection, the amazing Mrs. Lorillard—who gave such a vivid impression of magnetism and distinction.

To examine it more closely, Mary lifted the photograph in its massive, engraved, silver frame. What was it, even in this dead, flat counterpart, that gave to the lady the impression of supervitality? Mary did not know. Yet she was aware at once of the abundant sex-appeal in this lithe creature's body, an appeal which had filtered through the lens, been caught on the negative, and finally been stamped perdurably on this sheet of paper. As

Adora returned, Mary replaced the picture on the mantelpiece.

It's a lovely room, she commented.

Do you like it? I wonder if it suits me? An interior decorator arranged it for me.

It's charming, but I think I'd prefer you in a Spanish setting.

Oh, the dining-room's Spanish. I'll show it to you presently. The furniture is so heavy I have to send for a piano-mover when I want the place cleaned!

I was admiring this photograph.

Pretty, isn't she?

She's more than pretty. She's beautiful. Who is it?

Adora regarded her with astonishment. Why don't you know? It's Lasca Sartoris.

So that's the famous Mrs. Sartoris. Ollie told me that she had come back.

Revived by this identification of the photograph, a host of memories raced through the girl's mind. Lasca Sartoris! Why, she was almost a legend in Harlem, this woman who had married a rich African in Paris and had eventually deserted him to fulfil her amorous destiny with a trap-drummer from a boîte de nuit. But the signs and portents had been with her even here, for her husband had expired of a stroke the night she disappeared, apparently quite ignorant of all knowledge of her peccancy, and when his will, executed several months earlier, had been read, it was discovered that she had inherited the bulk of his huge fortune. By the time she had come into this money, she had long since tired of the trap-drummer and had passed on to other interests. It could hardly be said that Harlem, generally speaking, had received the tidings of Lasca's wayward adventures with approval, even with equanimity, but those who knew her apparently liked her, and the rest perhaps, when she returned, so thought one of Mary's informants, would be won over by her money, her beauty, her wit, and her charm. She is certainly unconventional, this woman had told her, but she is also Lasca: to know her is usually to forgive her. Now that she had seen the photograph, Mary believed she could understand.

Yes, she's back. Adora was speaking once more. I forget how short a time you've lived here: it's only a little over two years, isn't it? Good God! . . . Adora's eyes appeared to be literally looking back into the past. . . . I can remember when there wasn't any Harlem, when we used to go to Marshall's on Fifty-third Street for a bite to eat and to listen to Florence. I can still remember that red and green wall-paper. I wish I had some like it now! . . . Adora sighed. . . . Well, they've had cabarets and cabaret entertainers since then, but I don't think any of them have quite come up to Marshall's and Florence! Perhaps it seemed better because I was younger. Baron Wilkins's place was downtown then, too. Poor Baron! I don't suppose you've ever heard of Sisseretta Jones, the Black Patti, or Ernest Hogan, or Williams and Walker, or Cole and Johnson. . . .

I've heard of them all, Mary replied, although mostly they came before my time, but I've seen Bert Williams and, of course, Rosamond Johnson. . . .

Well, poor Bob Cole is dead, and Hogan is dead, and George Walker and Bert Williams and Aida Overton. . . . A tear glistened in Adora's eyes. . . . They were all my friends. I've appeared with them all. Those were the days. New York will never see coloured shows like 'em again. Why, these young whipper-snappers today don't know anything about the profession . . . except how to dance the Charleston. Some of 'em can't even do that! You should have seen George Walker do the strut!

Well, Adora went on, it was in those days that I met Lasca. She came up from Louisiana. Her father was a country-preacher, one of the Camp-meeting kind. A shoutin' exhorter. You know, hell and brimstone, and the congregation moanin' no end. Amen! . . . Tickled with the recollection of one of these ceremonies, Adora gave vent to a hearty chuckle. . . . I'd just like to be hearing one now. . . . She wiped her eyes with her handkerchief. . . . You've never been South, have you, Mary?

No, Mary replied.

Well, Adora continued, Lasca began by teaching

school in the backwoods down in Louisiana—she was educated at Straight College at New Orleans—and then suddenly an uncle died—an uncle who had inherited property in Kentucky from some buckra relation with a conscience—and he left his land to her. Now Lasca was always musical—she played the harmonium at her father's meetings—and when she got her money she came to New York to study.

You know what usually happens when you've been brought up in a minister's family: when you get the chance you cut loose and go to the devil. Well, Lasca certainly cut loose, but in the old days she never quite went to the devil. She always kept a certain dignity. Often I've seen her cut loose at Marshall's—she was just a kid then—towards three in the morning, do an old-fashioned pigeon-wing or a hoe-down—she'd learned all the Southern country-dances on the old plantations. She was good at the new ones, too, the turkey trot and the bunny hug. And when she got through dancing, she'd sit down to the piano and sing a shout or a lively Spiritual.

How did she get to Paris? Mary inquired.

This fellow Sartoris came over here on some French government mission or other; you see he was an official from one of the French provinces. The first time he set eyes on her he fell and they were married right away. He was an old man when she married him, and I don't believe she ever cared much for him, but Lasca knows what she wants and goes after it, more than most of us do.

That girl's got a positive genius for going after things.

Hasn't she been back here before? Mary asked. It seems to me . . .

You're right. She has. Many times, but let me see, I don't believe she's been back in the last two years . . . Adora pondered . . . How long has it been since Bert Williams died?

Mary shook her head and smiled. I can't tell you that, she answered.

Well, that's the last time Lasca was here.

Why does she come back at all?

God knows! Probably she gets bored. If I were Lasca I'd stick to Paris. No colour prejudice there, and what a spot to parade her particular line of material! But here—well, she shocks 'em. Certain people won't even have her in the house. She always raises hell here, without intending to, I guess. She just can't help it. She's just naturally full o' pep and she bounces the papas off their rails . . . Adora scowled . . . She'd better leave mine be. If she don't there'll be some fancy carvin' . . . Adora cut a scar in the air.

You know, Adora went on, Lasca did just what I wanted you to do, but you went back on me. Of course, Rannie's not cultured like Sartoris, but I'll bet he's got ten times the cash. You could do anything in Harlem you wanted to with that bunch of coin.

But I'm not Lasca, Mary protested. I'm afraid

I wouldn't be much of a success at that sort of thing.

Well, Rannie liked you, Adora said, liked you from the first moment he met you in my house, swore you were just what he was looking for . . . Suddenly, she fixed Mary with a gaze full of suspicion . . . You're not sore on account of anything you've heard about Rannie? she demanded.

No, I'm not sore at all, Mary replied. I just don't happen to love him, that's all.

That's all right: I get you when you talk about love. I couldn't marry either, if I wasn't in love. The trouble is that I have to pay for a lot of my love, like Rannie. You see these boys all know I cleaned up big in the theatre and when I want something, well . . . I guess it's worth it . . . sometimes. I don't know. She sighed. . . . Of course, she continued, Rannie didn't care whether you loved him or not. He wanted a respectable woman for a wife, somebody to give him a decent show-window, so he could go about a little more with the real swells. He thought you were the article. He's dead cut up about it.

I'm sorry, Mary responded. I can't help it. I just couldn't do it.

There, dearie! Adora crossed the floor, bent over and kissed her friend. There, we'll forget it.

The front door was heard to open and close. Presently, footsteps, slow and deliberate, resounded on the stairs; Alcester Parker slunk into the room.

Hello, 'Dora. Afternoon, Mary. He had a sheepish air.

Where've you been? Adora demanded sternly.

Just down to the pool-parlour, playin' with Irwin.

Well, you've been gone a long time, Adora whined. I looked for you when I went out.

I just been down to the pool-parlour, Al repeated dully.

Well, go on upstairs. I'm talking to Mary now.

With silent alacrity the boy obeyed her.

As he disappeared at the turn of the stairs, Adora burst into tears.

My life's nothing but dust and ashes, she sobbed. They all treat me like that, like dirt. They go and they come and they never think of me, and when a young, pretty flapper comes along . . . I don't deserve it, she cried. I try to get even by treating *them* like dirt, but it don't work. They listen to me shout, but they don't pay no attention.

They? Mary queried.

Well, he, Adora stammered. I mean Al. No, I don't! No, I don't! she cried. He'll never leave me! He's different! Al loves me!

Five

What was it in herself, Mary wondered, that held her aloof, prevented her from actually engaging her affections? She was certain that she was not a mental prig. Was there the possibility of being a physical prig? She enjoyed going to the theatre with young men; she liked to dance with them, to talk with them, and yet an indefinable something in her makeup interfered with the progress of a more intimate relationship. She was acquainted with many empty-headed boys, sheiks, they called them in Harlem, boys about whom most of the girls were mad, boys whom married women quarrelled over, silly, conceited boys who thought of nothing but their conquests and probably spoke freely about them among themselves. These, assuredly, were not for her. The more serious-minded young men in her circle of friends were naturally quite a different matter. Howard, for instance, was her kind, but she realized that she could never consider marrying Howard. Anyway Howard belonged to Ollie, and the others like him had never actually proposed to her. It was something in herself that didn't want them to propose to her that kept them from it, she was beginning to believe.

She cherished an almost fanatic faith in her race, a love for her people in themselves, and a fervent belief in their possibilities. She admired all Negro characteristics and desired earnestly to possess them. Somehow, so many of them, through no fault of her own, eluded her. Was it because she was destined to become an old maid, a bitter-minded spinster like Hester Albright? Yet even Hester subconsciously felt her birthright. She had seen Hester fall under the sway of Negro music that evening at her home. On many other occasions she had observed this phenomenon! How many times she had watched her friends listening listlessly or with forced or affected attention to alien music, which said little to the Negro soul, by Schubert or Schumann, immediately thereafter losing themselves in a burst of jazz or the glory of an evangelical Spiritual, recognizing, no doubt, in some dim, biological way, the beat of the African rhythm.

Savages! Savages at heart! And she had lost or forfeited her birthright, this primitive birthright which was so valuable and important an asset, a birthright that all the civilized races were struggling to get back to—this fact explained the art of a Picasso or a Stravinsky. To be sure, she, too, felt this African beat—it completely aroused her emotionally—but she was conscious of feeling it. This love of drums, of exciting rhythms, this naïve delight in glowing colour—the colour that exists only in cloudless, tropical climes—this warm, sexual emotion, all these were hers only through a mental understanding. With Olive these qualities were instinctive; also with Howard; even with Hester, to some extent; Adora throbbed with this passionate instinct—that was the real reason Mary's heart went out to her. Why, Mary asked herself, is this denied to me?

We are all savages, she repeated to herself, all, apparently, but me! She recalled what she had once been told—and her reason informed her that it was probably the truth—that Negroes never premeditate murder; their murders are committed under the reign of passion. If one made a temporary escape from a man bent on killing, it was likely to prove a permanent escape. The next morning, in another mood, probably he would have forgotten his purpose. There never had been, her informant assured her, a Negro poisoner. Negroes use the instruments that deal death swiftly: knives, razors, revolvers.

If she could only let herself go, revel in colour and noise and rhythm and physical emotion, throw herself into the ring with the others, figuratively shouting and hurling their assegais! But it would not be me, she argued with herself. Unless I acted naturally like the others, it would be no use. I must be myself. Perhaps, later, this instinct will come, awaken belatedly in me.

Preparations for Olive's wedding were progressing rapidly. Olive, as expert with the needle as with the cook-stove, spent much of her spare time sewing. She was making a trousseau that would be the envy of many a girl who had all the money in the world to spend on one: delicate chiffon and linen undergarments, embroidered and hemstitched, gay with lace, ribbons, bows, and insertion, together with a rainbow array of dresses. Olive's father had sent her a cheque for one hundred and fifty dollars with which to purchase materials for this wardrobe, a sum that would go a long way when one knew where to buy remnants or when one attended the sales advertised by the big department stores.

She sewed most of the time Howard visited her in the evenings, talking to him with her mouth full of pins or while she actively plied the needle. Sometimes she would toss him an end of flimsy material to be held taut while she divided it neatly with her long pair of shears. This action would naturally conclude with an embrace, a passionate kiss. Occasionally, Mary would accidentally stroll into the sitting-room in time to see this. Not that it mattered to them—before her they felt no self-consciousness—but it mattered to Mary who saw more than they intended, more, perhaps, than they were aware of. She saw that Howard was Olive's man and that she was his woman. It was more than a marriage; it was a primitive consecration. She saw that each would fight—kill if need be—to retain the other's love. This realization made her feel her own lack more keenly than ever. How had she, during the centuries, lost this vital instinct?

Her memory returned to her childhood days, to her mother and father. Her mother's father had been a freed slave who had been given a slice of land together with the custody of his own body. On this land he had prospered sufficiently to send his daughter to Fisk. Before she had married William Love she herself had taught school. The thought of her father almost invariably brought affectionate tears to Mary's eyes. To her he was an example of how perfect a man might be: straight, handsome, tall, distinguished, honest and upright, just and intelligent: his countenance and bearing reflected his character. Sweet and gentle he was too, and yet, Mary still remembered with a little thrill how the mere reading in a newspaper of an account of a lynching in Georgia, a particularly ghastly lynching, had thrown him into such a fit of rage that he had seized his revolver and started to leave the house, threatening to kill the first white man he encountered. She recalled how her mother, moved, too, beyond her bent, had experienced the greatest difficulty in persuading him to relinquish his purpose, employing, indeed, every weapon of persuasion at her command, even resorting to what little physical force she possessed. He had not gone. The revolver had dropped from his relaxed finger-tips, and the patient, resigned expression she knew so well had returned to his eyes. Mary was five years old when this had happened, but she could still remember the anguish in her mother's tone as she had implored her to go to bed, and the grey, ashen pallor in her mother's face, as she sank, exhausted after her successful struggle, into an armchair. They had never referred thereafter to this incident, but Mary would never forget it.

Her father, reared in a small town in the Middle West, had attended white schools, first the local public schools, later the state university. Early in life he had become imbued with the ideal of doing something for his unfortunate race. Later, this ideal became a passion which drove him on until, when he had accumulated sufficient money through his law practice to make his family comfortable and to educate his daughter, he devoted as much of his time as possible to public speaking, explaining the problems of the Negro to white audiences or fostering ideals of industry and ambition in the younger generation of coloured people.

Mary adored her father and it was with a feeling of pride and joy that she had learned from one of his recent letters that he planned to make one of his rare visits to New York. He arrived one morning early in October. Mary was unable to meet him at the station, as she could find no one willing to substitute for her in the library. Mr. Love, therefore, carried his bags to the home of Aaron Sumner, where he had been invited to be a guest, and then paid a call on his daughter at the library.

Dad dear! Mary greeted him.

He kissed her affectionately. They were very close to one another, this pair. Mary regarded him—she never tired of admiring him: he was tall, light brown, with short, curly grey locks, and a grey moustache. His nose was aquiline; his cheek-bones high and well-carved. Sometimes, in a spirit of beneficent fun, Mary called him Othello. He actually represented her idea of a Moor. Might he not, indeed, be one? The old slave traders were none too particular concerning the individuals they kidnapped along the African coast. A slave was a slave and a white man brought as much as a black. Not only were the miserable human beings raped from all parts of Africa, representatives of widely differing African tribes, but also Arabs, Egyptians, Moors, and even Spaniards and Portuguese were gathered in. In America these curiously distinct races came together and bore children; further, these children were often impregnated with French, Spanish, English, and Indian blood. The result, whatever the percentage of the mixture, was known in this enlightened country as a Negro and shared all the prejudice directed towards the full-blooded African.

How is mother? Mary asked. They sat in a small chamber adjoining the reading-room.

Fine, her father responded, and very envious of me, because she wants to see you so badly herself.

Why didn't you bring her, dad?

Well, it's a long and expensive trip, and I shall be here myself only a couple of days. You see, I had the excuse of my lecture in Newark. I hope you can come out to visit us next summer.

In the evening Mary was invited to dine at the Aaron Sumners'. She always delighted to go to this house: it had such an agreeable, comfortable air, without being luxurious or arty. You sank so deeply into the upholstered divans and easy chairs. The Persian carpets were thick and pleasant to walk on. The electric lamps were shaded in soft colours and the rows of books and the few pictures had all been selected with the design of making the place livable. This design was eminently successful.

Born in Georgia, of well-to-do parents, Mr. Sumner had been educated at Fisk where, during his senior year, he was fortunate enough to become acquainted with a young, Northern white man who had come down to investigate the institution, before donating a considerable sum towards its maintenance. A little later, he had sent for Mr. Sumner to offer him a responsible position in his business in New York. From trusted employee, Mr. Sumner, gradually securing the complete confidence of his friend, had eventually acquired an interest in the business. Mrs. Sumner was the daughter of a Philadelphia caterer who long ago had assembled a modest fortune. She, as a consequence, had been educated in a French convent. She had followed her father's example by sending her own daughters to Paris to school.

Mary came a little early, as she wanted to enjoy a talk with her father before the others arrived. When the first guest was announced, Mrs. Sumner joined them in the drawing-room. Slightly past forty, she was still a handsome woman; she had always possessed distinction of manner. She bought all her clothes in Paris, a city she visited at least once a year, usually in the spring when she could accompany her daughters back to New York. This evening she wore a frock of ecru crêpe which exactly matched the colour of her superbly formed shoulders so that, at a little distance, her back appeared to be entirely nude. A long chain of chrysoprase depended from her throat.

She was followed by Gareth Johns, the novelist. Mary noted immediately that the middle-aged man, with white hair, was nervous. Evidently it was his first appearance as a dinner-guest in a Negro home and he was attempting, not entirely successfully, to be easy in his manner.

What a charming place you have, Mrs. Sumner, he began, in rather a high key, from which the note of astonishment was not entirely lacking.

We find it comfortable, Mrs. Sumner replied, adding, I want you to meet Miss Love, and her father.

Delighted, I'm sure. Gareth bowed.

It's certainly a pleasure to meet you, Mr. Love

responded. Are you stopping in New York this winter? I always think of you as living in Paris.

I do live abroad most of the time, Gareth explained, but this winter I've taken a house near Stamford. You see, I'm trying to write a book about America.

I enjoyed Two on the Seine, Mary said, and it was very popular at the library. At one time I think we had fifteen copies. They're all worn out now.

Gareth looked bewildered.

It's so difficult to work in New York, Mrs. Sumner remarked. I don't wonder you chose the country.

It is better, and very convenient, only an hour from town, Gareth said.

At this juncture, Galva Waldeck, the concert singer, and Léon Cazique, the new secretary to the Haytian consul, arrived. During the introductions the maid appeared with cocktails and a plate of little, round slices of bread spread with caviare and sprinkled with egg-crumbs.

I loved your exhibition, Mary, Galva exclaimed, as she sipped her cocktail. Then, turning to Cazique, Mlle. Love—I always feel like saying Mlle. Amour, Mary—a organisé une exposition épatante de sculpture africaine.

Comme c'est intéressant, the secretary responded. J'ai vu plusieurs œuvres de ce genre l'été passé à Bruxelles. Elles étaient authentiques. Vous savez, peut-être, que les Allemands ont copié beaucoup ce genre de sculpture ces temps derniers. Les imitations sont si bien faites que l'on peut à peine les distinguer des vraies.

Je le sais, et c'est pourquoi j'ai refusé beaucoup d'exemplaires, Mary explained. Je crois que nous n'en exposons que des authentiques.

By Jove, I'd like to have seen that exhibition! Gareth cried. I didn't hear about it.

They haven't gone back to the owners yet, Mary assured him. Come to the library any day and I'll be glad to show them to you.

May I come tomorrow and bring Mrs. Lorillard?

I'd be delighted. I shall be there all day.

How is Campaspe? Mrs. Sumner inquired.

Oh, 'paspe's splendid, Gareth replied. She tells me I'm to have the pleasure of dining with you there next Thursday.

I'm so glad you're included. . . . Mrs. Sumner set down her untouched cocktail. . . . I don't know whether we should wait for Dr. Lancaster. Perhaps he's keeping C. P. T.

Mr. Sumner turned to Gareth. It's almost a joke among our group, he said. We're all inclined to be late. We've even got a legend about it. It seems that when the trumpet blew announcing the Judgment Day, white people turned out of their graves and went immediately to heaven. Two days later, angels seated on the pearly walls saw dense, black clouds arising in the West and hurried back to give the alarm that a terrific storm was on its way.

Oh no, St. Peter reassured them, that's only the coloured people coming to Judgment.

You're not unique in that respect, said Gareth.

My dear, Mr. Sumner went on to his wife, I don't think we'd better wait two days for Dr. Lancaster.

The ringing of the bell made it unnecessary to arrive at any decision in the matter.

There he is now, Mrs. Sumner announced, and we'll go in to dinner as soon as he takes his coat off.

The dining-room was a large ivory and blue chamber. The table was laid with rich silver and porcelain over a lace spread. In the centre, reflected in a mirror, stood a bowl of engraved blue glass from which a cluster of dahlias raised their magenta heads.

Mary was seated between Gareth Johns and Dr. Lancaster. She had never met either of them before this evening. The physician lived in Washington and, like Mary's father, was in New York on a visit. To all intents and purposes, he was as white as Gareth. His hair was a fiery red.

The conversation at first was general. Mr. Sumner spoke of Hayti, out of courtesy for his guest in the diplomatic service. This led to some discussion of the situation in the Virgin Islands.

It seems curious, Mr. Sumner averred, that the French, coloured Hayti and the Danish, coloured Virgin Islands should be dominated by an American navy government with all the prejudices of white Southerners.

I hear that the strict application of the Eighteenth Amendment—at least its *official* application—is destroying one of the Islands' greatest sources of revenue, Mr. Love remarked.

Do you mean to tell me, Gareth demanded indignantly, that that ridiculous law is being enforced on our dependent possessions?

Quite so, Mr. Sumner assured him, probably more rigidly than it is in New York City.

I visited the Virgin Islands once, Mr. Love continued. You know they're named after the eleven thousand that travelled about with St. Ursula. You see, Columbus landed there on St. Ursula's Day.

> She said, My dear,
> Upon your altars,
> I have placed
> The marguerite and coquelicot,
> And roses
> Frail as April snow;
> But here, she said,
> Where none can see,
> I make an offering, in the grass,
> Of radishes and flowers.
> And then she wept
> For fear the Lord would not accept,

quoted Mary.

So you know Wallace Stevens! Gareth cried with enthusiasm.

Not all by heart, but that, and Peter Quince at

the Clavier, and The Emperor of Ice-Cream, and . . .

Tea! Gareth interrupted. Oh, do, for my sake, recall Tea!

> When the elephant's-ear in the park
> Shrivelled in frost,
> And the leaves on the paths
> Ran like rats,
> Your lamp-light fell
> On shining pillows,
> Of sea-shades and sky-shades,
> Like umbrellas in Java.

Will you have any more of the fish? Mrs. Sumner inquired.

Gareth became aware that a servant with a heavy platter was bending over him.

I don't think I can refuse anything so good, he responded.

Dr. Lancaster took advantage of this diversion to speak to Mary.

Have you ever been in Washington, Miss Love? he asked.

No, never. I've always wanted to go, but there has never been an occasion.

Well, our life down there is varied and pleasant. There's always somebody or other from Howard if you want a game of bridge or a pleasant chat, but it's surely more interesting here. Harlem . . .

Mary smiled mischievously. I know what you're going to say: the Mecca of the New Negro!

Perhaps I was, he responded. Isn't it?

I suppose so; only we—some of us—get awfully tired of hearing about it.

To us on the outside, it seems magnificent, a dream come true, the doctor continued, sipping his Sauterne. A Negro city almost as large as Rome! We couldn't have counted on that a few years ago. You have everything here: shops and theatres and churches and libraries . . .

And cabarets, added Mary. You should have mentioned them first.

Well, they are an essential part of our life, I suppose. I think I must take in one or two before I return to Washington. Do you know, it's been years since I've visited a cabaret . . . He paused and with his fork pushed a mushroom across his plate . . . I've lived rather an odd sort of life altogether.

She regarded him with interest, but remained silent.

You can see that I might have joined the Blue Vein Circle. This fact has led me into some strange adventures. A good deal of my youth I spent among whites, passing . . . Later, I reverted to the other. On the whole, I prefer it.

I was sure you would, Mary replied.

The curious thing is this, he went on meditatively,

and I've never met any one else who felt just that way; perhaps no one else has gone through just my set of experiences—the curious thing is this, he repeated, that when I'm living with whites I have a white psychology and when I live with Negroes I have a Negro psychology.

Mary stared at him. And you say you've never met any one else like that? she demanded.

Not exactly. You see, it goes even deeper. There are occasions when I'm torn between the two, confused.

Mary was silent. She looked around the table. Galva Waldeck was conversing in French with Léon Cazique. Gareth Johns and Mrs. Sumner were engaged in an animated discussion.

No one? Mary repeated her question in a lower tone.

Well, I don't suppose I could really be sure what any one else felt. What I mean is, perhaps, that no one has confessed such a feeling to me.

As Gareth turned to her, Mary felt an unaccountable sense of relief.

We're discussing Rosamond Johnson's new book of Spirituals, he explained. I haven't seen it yet.

Do you like Spirituals? Mary inquired.

I dote on 'em. Mrs. Sumner wants me to hear Stand still, Jordan.

It's a wonderful song, Mary said. You should hear Taylor Gordon sing it.

I seem to be woefully ignorant, Gareth replied. He turned to Mrs. Sumner. Who's . . . ?

Mary was listening to Cazique across the table: Proust ressemble à un cours d'eau, un vaste fleuve qui, comme le Nil, jaillit dans plusieurs endroits, s'affermit dans sa course, embrasse des villes et des iles, et finalement se joint à un fleuve énorme et se précipite dans la mer!

Well, I'll get it tomorrow. . . . She was listening to Gareth again. . . . Do you know, he went on wistfully, I think I'd like to write a Negro novel.

Mary laughed. Everybody seems to be doing that. Have we become so interesting?

Some day, Dr. Lancaster was saying, perhaps a Negro will write a novel about white people.

I'd like to see that done, Gareth said.

It has been done, said Mary.

I suppose you mean Dumas, suggested Dr. Lancaster.

Or Pushkin, Gareth offered.

No, I mean by an American Negro, Charles W. Chesnutt. He's written several novels from a white point of view.

Never heard of him, said Gareth in amazement. Suppose you tell me some of the titles. He produced a pencil and a slip of paper.

Presently, Mrs. Sumner rose. We'll have coffee in the library, she announced.

In comfortable chairs before the fire, conversation continued over coffee, and later, over whisky and soda.

You seem to read more up here than any one downtown does, Gareth remarked to Mary. I don't see how you find the time.

It's my business, you see.

Yes, but the others . . . You were telling me you have calls for Aldous Huxley.

To be perfectly frank, most of the customers prefer A. S. M. Hutchinson.

Well, that's more human, Gareth said. I was beginning to be afraid you were paragons.

A bell tinkled.

That must be Robert Kasson's son, Mrs. Sumner announced. You know Robert Kasson of Philadelphia, she interjected to Galva Waldeck. Byron's just arrived in New York, like Dick Whittington, to make his fortune.

I hope he's brought a cat! cried Galva.

I don't know about the cat, but he may have brought a typewriter. His ambition is to become an author.

Mary's hands were trembling. Her heart was thumping. At this instant the door swung open and he stood framed in the doorway.

After the introductions he came straight towards her.

This must be fate, he said. This is the first day

I've been in New York since I met you at that orgy on Long Island, and here I run into you directly.

Mary smiled. Are you complaining? she inquired.

Ignoring this query, he lifted her hand. I was sure of it, he cried. You have fingers like the petals of a golden chrysanthemum. I've always remembered your fingers.

Mary felt too embarrassed to invent a reply.

Gareth Johns was still sitting near Mary. Apparently, Mr. Kasson, you have a talent for phrases, he commented. I hear that you are a writer.

Not quite yet, Byron responded. I want to write, but it's a large order, isn't it? It's difficult to begin when one realizes what you have accomplished.

So you've been reading my books.

Everybody reads your books, Mr. Johns.

Well, don't let that bother you. The critics and the public always like the new men best. They get tired of us old fellows, once they have discovered the secret of our formulas. What are you going to write about?

I don't know, Mr. Johns, that's just it. How does one go about writing?

Well, to be frank, I've always thought that the best way to go about writing was to write. You have plenty to write about. Gareth swept his eyes around the room.

I don't see any sense in writing about this, Byron protested, rather hotly, Mary thought. It's too much like Edith Wharton's set.

Well, the low life of your people is exotic. It has a splendid, fantastic quality. And the humour! How vital it is, how rich in idiom! Picturesque and fresh! I don't think the Negro has been touched in literature as yet.

I'm afraid I don't know very much about the low life of my people. Byron's tone was cold.

There's the college life . . .

I went to a white college. Byron turned away.

I seem to have offended your friend, Gareth said to Mary. I wonder how.

Oh, no you haven't. It's just because he's embarrassed at meeting a great author. Mary was surprised to find herself defending Byron. You see, he's probably never before faced a real novelist.

Shrugging his shoulders, Gareth lighted a cigarette.

I wonder, he said, if we could persuade Miss Waldeck to sing Stand still, Jordan?

Six

It was perhaps a striking coincidence that Mary should encounter Randolph Pettijohn the next day on her way to Craig's where she was accustomed to eat her lunch. Assuredly the incident caused her less embarrassment than she would have believed possible. Something had happened to give her a protective armour. What it was she did not attempt to discover. She only knew that she felt more secure, and when the King stopped to offer her his hand she grasped it almost sympathetically. She was sorry for Randolph Pettijohn and a little bit sorry for herself, too, because she was not ingenuous enough to accept what he only too evidently wanted to give her. It was plain to be seen that her rejection of his proposal had bewildered him; it had been a severe blow to his pride, had confused his previous estimate of mankind: she could sense that much. Not by what he said—as a matter of fact, he said nothing of any importance—but by his manner of saying it. It gave her a thrill of pleasure, made her self-consciously proud, to realize that this man respected her even more now that she had thwarted his desire. She passed on, feeling a trifle self-righteous, even vainglorious, until, analyzing her mood, her ultimate sense of humour got the better of her, advising her thuswise: Take no credit to yourself for your actions. You've only done what you couldn't help doing. You did not resist temptation when you refused Randolph Pettijohn. Quite the contrary.

As a consequence of these revealing reflections, Mary felt more humble as she entered Craig's, and, after nodding to one or two acquaintances, sat down at an unoccupied table. She determined not to wait for her father, whom she had invited to join her. He was constitutionally incapable of keeping an engagement on time. In fact, he had no sense of time at all, but, in self-defence, he often laughingly assured her that this trait was so typical of his race that he almost regarded it in the light of a sacred obligation to encourage it in himself.

As Mary lifted a spoonful of soup to her mouth, she was conscious of voices behind her.

Sylvia had no business to take her in.

Sylvia's only getting what she deserves. Look how she's been carrying on with Rumsey Meadows . . . Mary recognized Sergia Sawyer's voice.

Do you think she notices?

No, if she did, she'd have Lasca's life. She's very handy with a gun. Didya ever hear about . . . ?

Why, Mary wondered, as the conversation became too low for her to catch its drift, was she for ever hearing this woman's name? She began to cherish a certain curiosity in regard to this exotic figure. Why had she not met her? Would she like her when she did meet her?

Mary had finished her soup. Opening a book she had brought with her she began to read. Presently the waitress served her eggs. . . . She was almost through with her lunch when her father arrived.

I couldn't wait, dad, she apologized. Have to get back to the library.

I understand, he assured her. I didn't realize it was so late. I never know the time.

You carry a watch.

He smiled. Do you know, my dear, I never look at it. When I think of it at all it is as a piece of jewelry, a big diamond or something like that.

Dear old dad. She patted his hand. Then, What are you doing this afternoon?

I want to visit one or two of the schools, and I expect to see Professor Deakins of Howard. He's up here for the day.

What a time they're having at Howard! Mary sighed.

That's exactly what I want to discuss with him. I want to get his point of view about the muddle. It's hard enough, he continued, for us to get along among ourselves, but when white men are mixed up in our problems, it's well-nigh impossible. You're looking brighter, Mary. I thought you seemed a little tired last night.

Do you think so, dad? I'm feeling wonderful today. You know the old song:

> Got the world in a jug,
> Stopper's in my hand.

That's me!

I like to hear you talk like that.

I was a little worried last night, she admitted.

What was the trouble, Mary?

I don't know. A mood, I guess. I threw it off.

Don't worry, Mary. It doesn't do any good. Just knocks the machine out of gear.

I know it does, but some days I get the blues and they stick. She glanced at the watch on her wrist. . . . It's nearly two o'clock. I'll have to go back. . . . Drawing on her cloak, she kissed her father. . . . Remember I'm going to Newark with you tonight, Othello!

An hour later she felt she couldn't bear it if she had another inquiry for A. S. M. Hutchinson or Zane Grey. She made it a point of honour to try to encourage the young patrons of the library to improve their taste in reading, but her efforts in this direction on this particular day had all proved futile. Again and again, she had suggested a volume by Sherwood Anderson or Norman Douglas, but her suggestions had been received with indifference, if not with open hostility. Patiently, for the tenth time within the hour she recommended Jean Toomer's Cane to a youth who listened to her with apparent sympathy, but who hardly waited for her to conclude before he said, Ah guess Ah wants Duh Mine Wid Duh Iron Do'.

It's out, she was delighted to be able to announce.

Well, ain't you got nothin' else by duh man dat wrote et?

She had. Stamping the boy's card, she passed him the well-worn volume.

As he turned away, she was aware, although she did not look up, that another figure had taken his place.

Hello! The tone was one of hearty diffidence, as if the speaker were pretending not to be quite sure of a welcome.

Oh, it's *you!* she exclaimed. I'm so glad to see you. I'm getting so tired of handing out trash that I'm in a frightfully bad temper. I need cheering up.

What do you want the public to read? Byron demanded.

Well, it would help my disposition some if I could send Jean Toomer's Cane out today.

I'll take it, Byron assured her. I've always wanted to read it.

You haven't a card, Mary protested. It isn't my book. I can't lend it to you personally.

Well, I'll get a card. How often can I change books?

Every day, if you like.

Good! That'll give me a chance to see you every day.

Mary laughed. You don't have to come here to see me. Besides I don't always sit at the distributing desk. Why don't you call on me at home?

Nobody asked me, miss, he said. I was hankering for an invitation.

You don't strike me, Mary went on, as the kind of person who ever waits for anything.

Get me right, he urged. I'm really very shy, just a kid from the country up here in your great big Harlem.

It's the City of Refuge.

He grinned. The Mecca of the New Negro! You see, I know all the passwords. Do you think I'm a New Negro?

Newest one I've seen.

Hope so. But I don't want to appear fresh.

Stand aside, young man, and let me give this girl her Zane Grey.

I'll get my card, he announced.

In a little while he was back. I had to mention a couple of property owners, he informed her. It seems they've got to inquire into my integrity and financial responsibility.

What's your rating in Bradstreet? she inquired.

Two bits.

Are you kind to animals?

If you want to know, ask me around to meet yours.

Haven't got any.

Well, there are two children in the house where I'm staying, run by a regular old timer from the South. She calls 'em Locomotive Ataxia and Dementia Præcox. *They* like me. They already call me Unc' Byron.

You're taking up a lot of my time. Good heavens, Mary added to herself, I'm becoming coy!

I want to take up a lot more. Mary, may I call you Miss Love?

Please do, Byron, she assured him, laughing.

When may I come to see you?

She considered her answer. Her father would not be leaving until the next day.

Tomorrow night, if you like.

He shook his head vigorously. I'll come around tonight and wait.

She was firm. Tomorrow night.

What time?

Oh, around nine.

I'll be there at six-thirty.

For the remainder of the afternoon Mary enjoyed an unaccustomed spirit of elation. Making no more uplifting suggestions to her clients, she passed out books automatically. About four-thirty Gareth Johns arrived with Campaspe Lorillard and it afforded her a special kind of pleasure to exhibit the collection of African wood-carvings to these appreciative people. Mrs. Lorillard, in departing, promised to return with Edith Dale.

The next evening found Mary in such a state of suppressed excitement that Olive spoke about it.

What in God's name is the matter with you, Mary? her friend demanded. It can't be possible that the new sheik that's coming tonight has upset you.

Mary denied the insinuation, but later, at dinner, with Howard present, Olive renewed the attack.

Mary's fallen at last, she announced. Her sheik is coming tonight. I think we'd better go out, she added significantly.

Who is he, Mary? Howard inquired.

Ollie's talking nonsense, Mary protested. It's a man I've known a *long time*. His name is Byron Kasson, she explained limpingly.

Never heard of him, Howard retorted. Where'd he come from?

Mary met him night before last at the Sumners', Olive explained. A long time, indeed!

Why, Ollie, how can you? I met him at Adora's last summer.

Well, this is really terrible! It must be serious. . . . Olive regarded her friend in amazement. . . . It's funny you never mentioned him to me.

I didn't know him very well *then*. Realizing that she was plunging deeper and deeper, Mary sought refuge in a change of subject. Have you seen Mamie Smith? she asked. She's at the Lincoln this week.

Whew! Howard tossed back his head and

laughed heartily. That's a pretty broad hint. Mary wants us to go to the Lincoln tonight.

I didn't mean that at all and you know it, Mary protested.

I can't get it, Olive mused, Mary falling for a sheik! Well, you'll never drive us out of this house till we've given him the once over.

I don't want you to go at all.

We'll decide what you want, Olive said severely. Howard, help me with the dishes. Mary's got to fix herself up.

I'm all ready now, Mary objected. Let me put on an apron and help you.

No you don't. Olive definitely rejected this proffer. You go back to your room and comb your hair some more. She's done her hair four times tonight already, she explained to Howard, and I know she's not satisfied yet.

Olive and Howard retired to the kitchen. Although they had closed the door, Mary could hear them talking and laughing. She knew they were discussing her and her affairs and it made her both furious and happy, furious because they were teasing her, happy to realize that there was some foundation for the teasing. She thought it might be just as well to make one more attempt to get her hair right.

An hour later she consulted her watch. It was nine-thirty. Almost simultaneously the bell rang, and she heard Olive open the kitchen door and cross the room to answer it. She listened for the expected voice. She was disappointed. It was Dick Sill. He retired to the kitchen with Howard and Olive. Even from her own room she could hear them laughing. They were telling Dick now. She tried, unsuccessfully, to read. She lifted the shade, and peered out of the window. The street was deserted. She arranged her hair once more. Then, following an impulse, she went into Olive's room and borrowed a few drops of Narcisse Noir for her handkerchief and the little hollows behind her ears.

The bell did not ring again till ten-thirty. Mary ran to answer it, but Olive was beforehand.

So you're the new sheik, Olive greeted him.

Do I look like one? he laughed, and then cried, Hello, Mary.

How are you? Mary asked him. Rest your coat and hat and meet Mr. Allison and Mr. Sill.

The two young men stood grinning in the kitchen doorway.

Glad to know you both.

Are you any relation to Robert Kasson? Dick inquired.

He's my dad.

I've heard about him. I used to go down to Philadelphia a lot.

Sit down, Byron, Mary invited.

Yes, for heaven's sake, everybody sit down, Olive echoed.

Did you go to Howard? Dick queried.

No. Pennsylvania. I wanted to try a white college. I've got to get along in a white world, he went on, and I thought it might help.

Did it?

How should I know?

Byron's going to be a writer, Mary remarked.

I want to write, but I've got to earn my living while I'm learning.

What've you got on your mind? Howard asked.

Oh, nothing in particular. I just want to make a living until I get a start with my pen.

You'll have a fine time among the ofays, Dick asserted bitterly.

What do you mean? Byron demanded.

Sort o' kept you in your place at college, didn't they?

Byron was silent.

Did they ask you to their parties?

No, Byron responded, adding, It wasn't so bad.

Well, it won't be so bad here either, just so long as you're just another Nigger and know your place, Sill declared. They'll give you your choice too. You can run an elevator or lift pianos.

Dick! Mary implored him.

It's the truth, cried Olive. Let him talk.

Oh, I don't mind. I've heard it all before, Byron said. I guess I can find something better than that to do. If I can't I'll try Harlem. I only thought I could make more money downtown.

Try Harlem, will you? Dick's lip curled cynically. I guess you won't find that much easier. Howard here is a lawyer, but the race doesn't want coloured lawyers. If they're in trouble they go to white lawyers, and they go to white banks and white insurance companies. They shop on white One hundred and twenty-fifth Street. Most of 'em, he added fiercely, pray to a white God. You won't get much help from the race.

Don't believe him, Byron, Mary cried. You'll get along. I'm sure you will . . . Her tone trembled with indecision.

Olive's eyes flashed. Why, Mary, she protested. Do you get along? Don't you get less salary than white girls and aren't white girls without half your experience or ability promoted over you.

It's true, said Mary quietly, but don't discourage him, please.

They don't discourage me, Byron replied. I'm full of life and pep and I'll get something to do. You'll see. I don't care very much what it is. I'm not proud.

Well, old man, said Howard, I wish you luck. We'll do all we can, all of *us,* but the others . . .

Don't they want a member of the race to get on?

Say, Dick inquired, where have you been living? They *do* not. You'll have to fight your own race harder than you do the other . . . every step of the way. They're full of envy for every Negro that makes a success. They hate it. It makes 'em wild. Why, more of us get on through the ofays than through the shines.

Now, Dick, you're laying it on pretty hard, Howard suggested.

Not a bit of it. I'll say more. Who supports Roland Hayes? Who supports Florence Mills? Is it white or black audiences?

After all, Dick, be fair, Olive objected. They've got more money, thesc others.

That's it, cried Howard, they've got more money. That's what I've always said: we've got to have money to fight the system and earn the respect of the world.

Where are we going to get it? Dick asked fiercely.

Bottle it, Dick, said Olive. You'd think this was a Marcus Garvey meeting. Let's not spoil the evening for Byron and Mary. Come along with Howard and me. We're going to the Lincoln to see Mamie Smith.

The show's over now, said Mary.

Well, anyway, Olive insisted, I want to go for a walk.

What about a cabaret? Howard suggested.

Great! cried Dick. Now you're talking. I'm dying to do the Black Bottom again with Ollie! She's the best dancer in Harlem.

Bottle it, Dick, Olive repeated, laughing.

As the door slammed behind the three departing, Mary sighed and settled back into the couch.

This is hard on you, she said. I'm sorry. You didn't come here to listen to a lecture.

Oh, that's all right, Byron assured her. I'm used to talk like this, only I haven't heard much of it lately. Since I've been going to college I'm sort of out of step with it, that's all. The boys I know at home, most of them, get on all right, he added frowning. Who was that fellow who was doing all the talking?

You mean Dick Sill?

Yes. Disgruntled, isn't he? What does he do?

He is a secretary for somebody or other downtown. He *is* disgruntled. He says he's going white.

Byron stared ahead of him. I couldn't do that. Could you?

No, I couldn't.

I wonder why they didn't ask us to go along with them to the cabaret?

They're engaged, Mary replied coldly. I suppose they want to be alone.

Engaged! I see. I don't wonder. . . . But the other fellow went along.

Wouldn't you like a cup of coffee? Mary asked him.

I'd love it, and I'll help you make it.

Pressing the burning tip of his cigarette against the surface of an ash-tray, he followed her into the kitchen.

It's a great place you've got here.

Mary was measuring the coffee. It is nice, isn't it?

Great! Luxury for me. I'm living in a dump.

Mary filled the pot with water. What kind of things do you want to write about? she inquired.

Oh, I don't know. You've got awfully pretty arms.

Have I? Haven't you anything definite in mind?

What everybody writes about, I guess. Love, and all that. I thought of writing a story about a coloured girl in love with a white boy and how he ditched her.

Madam Butterfly, Mary murmured. As she lighted the fire under the coffee-pot, she looked at him hard. Why don't you write about us? she demanded.

Us?

Yes, Negroes.

Why, we're not very different from any one else except in colour. I don't see any difference.

I suppose we aren't, Mary spoke thoughtfully. And yet figures stand out.

Figures?

Do you know anything about Christophe? It seems to me that the story of Christophe would make a gorgeous subject for a novel.

Who was Christophe?

They were seated on chairs in the kitchen, waiting for the coffee to boil.

Born and raised in slavery on the Island of Saint-

Christophe, later French General in Hayti, Christophe proclaimed himself Emperor in March 1811. He became Henry I, and was called the Black Napoleon. On a rising slope at the apex of a narrow ravine he built himself a palace—not unlike Louis's great palace at Versailles—which he named Sans Souci. He erected other dwellings and country-seats, Queen's Delight, The Glory, The King's Beautiful View, but his masterpiece was La Ferrière.

La Ferrière was a citadel constructed of blocks of stone thirty feet thick. Capable of harbouring thirty thousand soldiers, it raised its stern face at the top of a mountain on the border of a cliff that dropped sheer two thousand feet. At present the only approach to this citadel is an uncertain foot-path. Christophe erected this fortress as a protection against a possible French invasion of his Empire. It was guarded by brass cannon. It is still guarded by these cannon. The Haytian government has been offered large sums for them, and it would be perfectly willing to sell them, but no way has yet been devised of getting them down the mountain.

Christophe's way of getting them up, of getting up the huge rocks of which the citadel was constructed, was ingenious and simple. They were dragged up the cliff-sides and steep mountain passes by human hands. One day he watched a hundred men trying to haul a cannon to its resting place. Now and again they stopped to rest. These pauses were annoying to the Emperor. He dispatched a messenger to discover the reason for them. The labourers sent back word that the gun was too heavy for their strength and asked that they might be assisted by a hundred more men.

Commanding them brought into the royal presence, the Emperor ordered them to fall into line. Then he directed every fourth fellow to fall out. These were shot. He quietly informed the remaining seventy-five that he expected the cannon to be in its place before he had finished his luncheon.

Little progress was made. Two hours later they assured him that the task was impossible.

The Emperor laughed. Fall in, he commanded. . . . Every third man out. Guards, fire!

Now, he informed the cowering wretches, I will order every second man out next time. If the gun was too heavy for a hundred men, surely fifty will find it light.

They did.

On another occasion he grew cold to a former favourite. Strolling to the edge of the cliff with the fellow, he talked softly to him. Standing over the abyss, he bade the man leap. Reading no mercy in the Emperor's eyes, reading rather the horrible alternatives that awaited his refusal, he obeyed. By some chance the branch of a tree some twenty feet below broke his fall. With broken arm, his face bruised and bloody, he crept back to his master.

Sire, he said, I have done your bidding.

Christophe was laconic. Leap, he commanded. Six feet tall, of pure African blood, black as coal, Christophe's nature was violent and impatient of all restraint. Loving splendour and power, he created a court and a nobility. Bravery and humility failed to touch him. He had no mercy. He ruled for fifteen years. When at the end of that period, during a revolution, his body-guard deserted him, he rose, bade farewell to his wife and family, retired to his own chamber and blew out his brains. . . . The coffee's boiling. Get some cups out of the cupboard.

Mary arranged the tray, setting the ejaculating percolator on a blue tile, and preceded Byron into the sitting-room. Seating herself, she poured out the coffee while he made himself comfortable in a chair and lighted a cigarette.

I couldn't write about things like that, Byron said.

What sort of things did you write about in college?

Oh, you know, the kind everybody else does.

Did your professors like your work?

Well, they encouraged me. They said it was pretty good for a coloured man.

I remember you told me that before. You said it wasn't enough.

Of course, I want to do better than that! I want to write as well as anybody.

Of course, you do. Why don't you choose a subject that you know all about? Something about our people? she asked him again.

I don't know so much about our people that is different. I told you that. We are born and we eat and we make love and we die. I suppose we're just like the others.

I suppose we are, Mary replied, only we don't eat where we want to or die where we want to.

But we make love where we want to. . . . Joining her on the couch, Byron seized her hand.

Mary felt a strange, tingling sensation. It was as though a mouse had raced up her arm from her captured hand to her shoulder and descended by way of her spine.

Don't do that, she adjured him faintly.

Why not, Mary? He caressed her hand softly with his lips and as she did not repeat her request to desist—all power of resistance seemed to have deserted her—he held her close in his arms. Mary could no longer control her will. It was delicious, this drifting feeling that came over her. As her head fell back against his shoulder, his moist lips met her mouth.

I love you, he whispered, beautiful golden-brown Mary!

You do love me, Byron? You do love me? She wanted to hear him say it again and again.

He stopped her mouth with kisses, and these, too, were the whole of his reply.

Seven

When Olive came home, just as the grey dawn was spreading its pale, disagreeable light through the window, Mary was still awake, but she did not call out to her friend. She heard Olive tiptoe into her room and softly close the door. Later, she dozed a little. Before retiring, she had thought it safer to set the alarm-clock and she turned drowsily to its buzz at a quarter after eight. Then she tumbled out of bed to turn on her tub. Olive, she discovered, had already departed for the city.

As Mary started forth, the sun was shining brightly, and it seemed to her, walking rapidly down Edgecombe Avenue, that she descried happiness in every face. Tired as she was, after her sleepless night, her blood tingled with a warm glow of joy; she felt an uplifting, elating excitement. And Ollie had called her cold! Long in awakening, she had awakened vibrantly. Once from one of the high galleries of the Metropolitan Opera House she had listened to Siegfried, and she now recalled the glorious music that accompanied Brünnhilde's awakening in the last act. Like Brünnhilde, Mary too had been awakened by a kiss.

Nothing else mattered now; nothing else counted: she knew that. I'd steal for him; I'd kill for him! she admitted to herself. For him I'd give up my family, my friends, my position, everything!

At the library she had the sensation that every one was staring at her.

Why, Mary, what is the matter? Miss Langley, one of the white assistants demanded.

Realizing the implications of this query, Mary was slow to reply. Apparently, the world was aware when one was in love.

What do you mean, Alice? she parried.

You look as happy as a humming-bird who has found a new flower, Alice explained.

My Lord, what a morning! was the refrain which ran through Mary's head, a refrain with a new meaning. The stars, indeed, had begun to fall!

I am happy, Alice! she confessed. I am happy. I don't know why; I'm just happy.

Alice's glance, Mary noted, was quizzical. However, she took up her position behind the desk, and said nothing more.

Mary, too, began her morning's work. Automatically, without argument, she passed One Increasing Purpose over the counter to a young girl who had inquired for it. So far as Mary's present mood was concerned, it might just as well have been a copy of A Passage to India or Those Barren Leaves. She repeated this carefree gesture with many more books for which on another occasion she would have felt slight respect. In her subconsciousness, as a matter of fact, Mary began to harbour a slight suspicion in regard to the reliability of the literature of disillusion.

Byron's name, sung over and over again in her mind, began also to weave contrapuntally a pattern of pain in her heart. He had promised to telephone. Why didn't he keep this promise? She could not tolerate the knowledge, she was beginning to realize, that he should be somewhere else while she was here. She wanted him near her always. Was love like this, that you began to suffer the moment you experienced it? Why didn't he telephone? Was he so indifferent that he could sleep? Several times she heard the bell tinkle in the adjoining room. Twice, she sped across the floor to answer it, in spite of the fact that the instrument was on the wall two steps from the principal librarian's desk.

You must be expecting a call, Mary, was Alice Langley's comment.

After this remark, although it cost her an agony of impatience, Mary permitted the bell to ring until some one in the inner office lifted the receiver, but this happened so frequently that it seemed incredible that not one of the calls should be for her. Presently a new anxiety beset her: considering the unisolated location of the telephone, she would be unable to speak freely, to say what she wanted to say. What she principally wanted to say, she was now aware, was in the nature of a complaint: she desired to upbraid Byron for not calling her earlier. Was he, her succeeding despairing inner voice demanded, going to call her at all?

At noon she was so completely occupied with the irksome requirements of an offensively precise youth—he had brought in a long typewritten list of obscure volumes dealing with tribal magic, and it was almost with shame that Mary had to confess, after considerable searching in the card-catalogue, that the library could not supply a single one of them—that when the bell rang again she did not hear it.

Alice Langley prompted her: Miss Silbert has been calling you for some time. Telephone.

Mary hastily returned the list to the obnoxious youth, gave a vicious stamp to a girl's card on the desk before her, and slipped from her stool. She walked, conscious that Alice's curious eyes were following her, the length of the room. Her brow was molten lava, her hands were ice. In Miss Silbert's room she lifted the receiver to her ear.

Hello!

Is that you, Mary?

Yes.

My adored one, can't you say any more than that?

No, not now.

What's the matter? The voice became more importunate, even a trifle petulant. Don't you feel the same way you did last night?

Yes.

Then, what's the matter? Don't you love me, Mary?

Yes.

Then, why don't you say something?

I can't.

At last he seemed to comprehend. You're not alone?

No. How she hated this! Never again would she permit him to telephone her at the library. She felt Miss Silbert's accusing eyes creeping up and down her back. She knew what Miss Silbert was thinking: she knew what white people thought about Negroes under such circumstances. I'm going to Craig's to lunch at one o'clock, she added.

I'll join you there, he promised. Good-bye.

Good— Wait a minute! . . . but he had already hung up the receiver.

She returned to her position behind the counter. Alice was frankly staring at her now, making no slightest effort at dissimulation. A little later she saw Alice whisper to one of the other girls. The girl listened, giggling. Mary believed she was about to faint. She loathed Byron. In her present mood she felt she never wanted to see him again.

Miss Silbert was passing her desk. You don't look well, Mary, the librarian remarked sympathetically.

I've got a headache.

Alice, overhearing, grinned.

It must be the air in here, Mary hurried on. It's very close. I felt fine when I came in.

Miss Silbert's glance sought the secret in Mary's eyes, searched deep into her soul, Mary felt, but the librarian said nothing more.

One o'clock at last. Craig's. The same crowd. The same gossip, but today it seemed to have a new and unpleasant significance. They seemed to be talking about *her*. She caught phrases without names:

He went to see her last night. . . .

. . . creeper. . . .

Some sheik! Ha! Ha!

One-fifteen. Still Mary waited. As Byron had not arrived at one-thirty, she ordered lunch, only to discover when it was served that she was not hungry. The food revolted her, choked her. The vague chorus continued to buzz around her. The laughter bubbled.

At a quarter of two, as she was arising from her seat preparing to draw on her cloak, he came in. Her expression reproached him.

Hello, Mary, he greeted her.

I thought you were coming to lunch with me.

He seemed bewildered.

I didn't understand it that way. I'm sorry. Did you wait? I thought you meant for me to look in on you here.

You said you'd join me.

I couldn't eat anything. I only had my coffee about an hour ago.

She felt the tears rising, her gorge tightening. Here he stood before her, and yet she was not happy. She wanted. . . . What did she want?

I was talking from the librarian's room, she explained. It was difficult to say very much.

I got that after awhile, he said. At first I couldn't understand why you were so cold.

I must have sounded that way. I think, Byron, she went on, it would be just as well if you didn't telephone me at the library again.

All right, he replied. It was you who suggested it.

Why didn't you call me up earlier? she demanded almost fiercely.

Why, I didn't think you'd be around earlier. It was so late when I left last night.

I was at the library at nine. I'm always there by nine.

I didn't get up at nine. Say, are we quarrelling already?

I'm sorry, Byron dear. I guess I'm tired. I'm feeling very nervous this morning.

You poor darling! He squeezed her arm affectionately.

Don't do that here, Byron, she begged.

Well, what can I do? When and where can I see you?

Mary smiled wanly. I must seem like a fool, Byron.

Can I come around tonight?

Oh, what will Ollie think?

Do you care what Ollie thinks?

No—oo. Yes, come around tonight, Byron.

What time?

Oh, about eight-thirty.

I'll be there.

Mary felt happy and warm again,

Are you looking for work yet, Byron? she inquired.

He laughed uneasily. Why, I just got up. How could I look for a job this morning? Besides I want to take a little time to look around. I don't want to take the first thing that offers.

Later, after he had left her at the door of the library, she was frightened. Her inexperience, her prior lack of desire for experience, had tricked her. She had been, she assured herself, too forthright. She had permitted him to know at once that she loved him. In this respect, at any rate, she had been perhaps a daughter of her race, but vague doubts clouded her mind, forcing her to be uncertain whether she had been wise to yield so easily to this warm emotion. Could she never be simple? Apparently not. This troublesome brain of hers, standing a little apart and judging with calm dispassionate logic all that she did, informed her that she had allowed him to know too soon that she loved him; she had let him see her jealousy too soon, permitted him to learn how much she missed him when he was not with her. He must now, she mused, be fully aware of his power over her. Yet she understood that in the future she could hold herself no more in check. In yielding to her first passionate emotion, she had apparently forfeited her peace of spirit. She had been in love *consciously* less than twenty-four hours—she realized that although something important had happened to her the day she met Byron at Adora's it was nothing like what had happened to her now—and already she was tasting all the anguish and bitterness of this condition. She was no longer the mistress of her emotions. To all intents and purposes, she admitted, she was their slave.

Olive had not yet returned when Mary entered the flat that evening. Repairing to the kitchen she lifted the lid from several canisters—flour, sugar, spices, dried mushrooms, kidney beans: all mysterious ingredients. What did one do with them? In the ice-box she discovered half a cold roast of lamb reposing on a platter, a curious mixture with a pungent aroma in a bowl, a dish of pyrex glass two-thirds full of cold, scalloped potatoes. Olive, she knew, would be able to convert these substances into an appetizing meal, while she, Mary, was helpless. Sinking into a chair, she sighed.

The outer door opened and closed as Olive entered.

Mary! she called. Then, What on earth are you doing in the kitchen?

I thought I'd like to try to get dinner, but I don't seem to know what to do.

Olive regarded her silently for a moment: astonishment shone from her eyes. It was obvious, too, that she was amused.

You set the table, she commanded half-humorously, and I'll get dinner as usual.

But Ollie, I really want to learn how to cook. Please let me help.

Well, Olive remarked, as she tied an apron over her dress, the sheik is pretty good, I guess. Studying up on domestic science already, eh?

Mary could not resist a smile. The sheik *is* pretty good, she echoed, altering the stress. I thought that some night when he came here to dinner I'd like to prepare it.

You thought . . . ! Say, Mary, don't scare the man away. You prepare your first meal for him after you're married. It will be too late for him to leave you then.

Ollie, do you think I'll be as bad as all that?

I'll say you'll be rotten. . . . Olive's increased amazement was clearly written on her countenance. . . . When you get started, Mary, you're certainly a fast worker, unless you've been holding this sheik out on me. You haven't been meeting him in the Park for the past few months, have you?

Ollie! You know I haven't.

How late did he stay last night?

Oh, he must have left right after you went out.

Well, if he did, *he's* a fast worker too! What time is he coming in tonight?

Why, how . . . ? Eight-thirty.

Well, run along and get ready. It will take you at least two hours.

Howard was dining with them again. He and Olive were going to the theatre. They were merciful to Mary, sparing her further references to the subject on which she was sensitive.

I wish you'd been with us last night, Mary, Howard said.

Where did you go?

Atlantic City Joe's. We felt like slumming.

I never heard of the place. You know I'm not very crazy about cabarets.

I'd never been there before, said Olive. It seems to be a favourite dive of Dick's. There's a loose dancer called Zebra.

What a belly-wobble! cried Howard with enthusiasm. She sang a song which goes:

> Takes a better man than you
> To make sweet mama shout!

The whole place is about as big as this room, Olive went on, but there's really more space for dancing than there is at the Black Venus because they keep more of the floor clear. Dick is certainly a bear at the Black Bottom.

When, some time later, they arose from the table, Mary suggested to Olive, Please leave the coffee in the pot. I'll warm it up when I want it.

Company, eh? Howard murmured interrogatively.

Yes, Olive replied, in a tone that prohibited further inquiry.

After they had departed, Mary returned to her room to put on a clinging, blue silk dress, with no sleeves, and a skirt that fell only to her knees. She rearranged her hair. She made up her face and lips more carefully. Seeking the bottle of carbona from the bathroom cupboard, she removed a minute spot from one of her satin shoes. Then she looked at the clock. It was quarter to nine.

Mary discovered that she was sleepy. She had enjoyed so little rest the preceding night. She went to the kitchen and lit the fire under the coffee-percolator. Fancying the place was too warm, she opened the kitchen window. Then she lounged rather listlessly in a chair until the brown bubbles began to dance merrily in the glass dome of the percolator when she poured herself out a large cup of the stimulant and returned with it to the sitting-room.

She sipped the hot liquid with a spoon. Still restless, she went back to her room in search of cigarettes and a book. She examined the labels of many volumes on her table before she eventually chose David Garnett's The Sailor's Return. Back in the sitting-room, she slowly sipped her coffee, lighted a cigarette, and opened the book. Perfection is in unity; prefer one woman first, and then one thing in her: so read the first lines. She laid the book aside. What, after all, did she know about this man? Did Byron, she wondered, prefer one woman first? Was *she* first? Had there been others? Were there others now? Mary's blood pumped furiously from her heart as she thought what it would mean to her if he cared for another woman. She wanted him for herself and for herself alone. She wanted to possess him.

> Ah wants mah man to be mine alone,
> Cause Ah'm evil an' jealous down to duh bone . . .

She permitted herself to slip into a half-somnolent meditation in which she gave herself over to the bliss of imagining what life with him would be like. Suddenly, with a start, she became wide-awake. Consulting her watch, she discovered that it was a quarter of eleven. There was a draught in the room. She remembered the open window and closed it. Then she returned to her chair and began to read: The Duke of Kent came safe into Southampton Docks on the tenth of June, 1858. On board of her was a mariner named William Targett, returning to his own country as a passenger, having shipped at Lisbon. He was . . . Mary jumped at the sound of the bell. Then she sat quite still for a moment until she had regained some slight control of her twitching muscles. At last, she opened the door.

•was she not angry,
did She question him ?
why does the narrarater
end it like this.

Eight

You can't catch me!

I'll bet I can!

Mary sprinted down a path with Byron following hot after her. At the moment he was about to capture her, she made a swift turning to elude him, lost her balance, and fell. Stumbling over her prostrate form, Byron sprawled too. Lying prone on the cold ground, they screamed with laughter.

When they had recovered from their merriment, they walked hand in hand down the path until they discovered a bench on which they seated themselves. A squirrel, scrambling out of the dead leaves, crossed the path, pausing an instant in his passage to sit on his haunches and listen apprehensively, and scampered up a slender tree-trunk. A sparrow hopped up and down the gravel, pecking for worms. Now and then he cocked his head, chirped, and regarded the pair inquisitively.

Can you Charleston? Byron inquired unexpectedly.

Not very well, Mary replied. Can you?

For reply, he flung aside his overcoat, and leaped to the centre of the path where he began to execute a series of wild steps. Mary clapped her hands rhythmically.

You might have been on the stage! she applauded him.

I don't do it very well.

Where did you learn?

He laughed. You'd never guess. A couple of white fellows at college taught me. Sometimes I think that's how I got my degree.

It's nice here in the Park, isn't it?

I love it. Resuming his coat, he seated himself beside her and closed his palm over her hand.

How many days is it that we've been coming here together?

It must be several weeks, but every time seems like the first time to me.

Mary began to sing softly:

> Roses used to was
> So sweet, so sweet, dear.
> Sunshine used to was
> So bright, so bright.
> Now there ain't
> No roses nowhere, dear —
> Seems lak duh sun
> Done stopped a-givin' light,
> Cause you had to go away . . .

That's a good tune, but a bad sentiment. I'm not going away.

I'm not going away either, said Mary, so you won't have any occasion to sing it. I wonder if you would, she mused aloud.

Would what?

Feel that way if I went away.

I'd follow you.

She squeezed his hand.

After a moment she said, I've been walking in this Park for many months. When I get through my work at the library it's what I always want to do first. I think of it as *my* Park, and now I've led you into it.

We're just two babes in the woods, he exclaimed. Let's roll in the leaves and cover ourselves up and get lost together for ever.

I'd adore it, Mary responded. What would we eat?

Squirrels and sparrows.

Oh, not those cunning squirrels.

Nuts.

I don't believe there's a nut-bearing tree in the Park. I've never seen one.

Well, we'll have our meals sent in from Flo's!

That's better . . . and use the leaves for a tablecloth!

And blankets!

Mary sighed. I wish life were as simple as all that! Why isn't it?

It's wonderful anyway, Mary.

It's wonderful now.

Baby duck! It'll be even more wonderful later, after we are married. He began to sing:

A sweetie like you,
A sweetie like you
Can't belong to nobody but me!

How do you know?

Tease! Unfaithful already?

What about you?

Cross my heart. Yours till death do us part, he asseverated with mock solemnity. He went on with his song:

A sweetie like you,
A sweetie like you
Would fill me with misery,
Cause if you'd leave me
I'd feel so sad,
I'd be just like a sheik
Gone ravin' mad —
Like a darktown sheik gone . . .

Some sheik! she interrupted him, continuing in song:

Singin' Sam from way down South
Sounds lak he's got a organ in his mouth.

You darling!

Byron, there's a big dance next week for the United Coloured Charities.

Let's go.

I was waiting for you to ask me.

As if you ever had to wait for me!

Well, it seems to me I'm always waiting for you.

If we go to the dance we'll make the appointment for the night before and then perhaps we'll get there.

Don't scold me.

I'm not scolding you. Ah'm jes' nacherly lovin' you, mah honey.

I adore you when you talk like that. Makes me feel I'm your daddy!

Honey, you is, fo' sho'.

Where did you learn that delicious lingo?

Out of Jezebel Pettyfer and Porgy.

Glancing hastily up and down the path to be sure no one was approaching, he kissed her.

That was nice, Mary assured him.

Say thank you!

I didn't get enough to be thankful for.

He kissed her again.

Byron, don't please! Not so hard, dearest. You're mussing me all up.

I like to!

You talk like a savage!

I am. I'm an African cannibal! Son of a king! Going to eat you up for my dinner! Growling, he exposed his even, white teeth.

She shouted with laughter. I'm so happy, Byron, so very happy! Let's make it last always.

He responded with another tune:

Till summer leaves the jungle,
Till stars cease to shine,

Till the river Congo freezes,
Till then you'll be mine. . . .

Permitting her head to fall against his shoulder, she silently enjoyed the ecstasy of this position for a time before she suggested, It's growing dark, dear. I think we'd better start home.

I thought we were going to make this our home, he protested.

Well, I will if you want to, but I thought maybe you'd like some of Ollie's biscuits.

Tempter! You coax me with hot bread!

You're easily coaxed.

One more kiss!

No, you've had enough. Rising quickly, she dashed away from the bench, crying over her shoulder, Catch me then!

He captured her easily and claimed his reward.

They walked on rapidly, hand in hand, their faces radiant with happiness. Presently their way lay parallel with the bridle-path. On horses, a man and woman were slowly approaching. A brilliant arc-lamp overhead illuminated the faces. Mary regarded the woman who, in a severely cut, black riding-habit, sat astride her mount. The face was beautiful, but cold and haughty, tortured, too, Mary thought.

Suddenly her voice cut the silence, clear and chill. Every syllable could be distinctly heard.

Disgusting, she remarked to her companion, that they should permit Niggers in the park!

The pair, without looking back, rode on together.

Mary clutched at Byron's arm and bowed her head.

We were too happy, she moaned. It's a judgment.

Byron's lip was quivering. Mary, he stammered, I haven't told you all the things that have happened to me.

What do you mean?

Things like that.

Oh, she moaned. Why can't they leave us alone or take us in? Can't we live? Can't we breathe without being subjected to these insults? Looks! Words! I'd prefer the lash. Slavery! Well, we knew where we were then!

They started to walk away.

Mary, Byron said quietly, this sort of thing happens to me every day.

Poor boy! I was afraid to ask you.

I answer advertisements for clerks, for secretaries. I'm insulted by office-boys, even, he added bitterly, by our own people: porters, elevator boys. You's puttin' on ahs, you shine, one of them said to me the other day. Why doan you git down an' work where you belongs?

That's the worst, what our own people do, Mary said. Do you know that the Underwoods dined downtown with white friends last week, and the next morning the coloured servants left? They said they wouldn't wait on Niggers!

Sometimes they laugh! Byron went on, his voice choking.

They don't know, Mary consoled him, these others, they don't know what they're doing.

That makes it worse still, Byron cried passionately. I go into an office where a white boy or a white girl is sitting at the desk. What do *you* want? they demand superciliously. He won't see you. He don't want Niggers!

I went through it when I tried to get into the library, Mary confessed. At first no one would even see me. Not a single member of the board would grant me an appointment. Eventually, a letter which Mr. Sumner wrote to an influential friend won me a hearing. Now, to be perfectly frank, they're lovely to me, but they don't promote me. They promote the white girls.

What can we do? Byron demanded, clasping and unclasping his hands. Here we are in an alien world. We think, we feel. We do our best to fit in. We don't want *them*. All we want is to be let alone, a chance to earn money, to be respectable.

I believe, said Mary, that they actually prefer us when we're not respectable.

They walked up Seventh Avenue in silence. The streets were crowded with pedestrians, white and coloured, scurrying home from work. As they approached One hundred and twenty-fifth Street, the blacks began to predominate. Almost immediately after they had passed that thoroughfare they met only Negroes. They had crossed the line.

Nigger Heaven! Byron moaned. Nigger Heaven! That's what Harlem is. We sit in our places in the gallery of this New York theatre and watch the white world sitting down below in the good seats in the orchestra. Occasionally they turn their faces up towards us, their hard, cruel faces, to laugh or sneer, but they never beckon. It never seems to occur to them that Nigger Heaven is crowded, that there isn't another seat, that something has to be done. It doesn't seem to occur to them either, he went on fiercely, that we sit above them, that we can drop things down on them and crush them, that we can swoop down from this Nigger Heaven and take their seats. No, they have no fear of that! Harlem! The Mecca of the New Negro! My God!

Nine

Dancing parties, assuredly, were no novelty in Harlem. A night in which there was no opportunity to go to one might be counted as exceptional. There were, first, the modest rent-parties, to which little groups were invited to dance to the music of the phonograph in somebody's small apartment, individual contributions of fifty cents helping to defray the occupant's exorbitant rent. Similar small, informal dances in apartments were often given without expense to the participants, although it cannot be said that the hostess was likely to complain if one of the guests brought in a bottle of gin. Moreover, on any occasion when two or four wanted to dance, and had the money, they might visit a cabaret. Finally, at least once a week and not seldom twice, some society or institution or club arranged a ball in one or another of the larger halls. These naturally varied considerably in importance. The parties given by the theatrical set were small and more or less exclusive. The sporting set, too, interested in prize-fighting and gambling, pretty much flocked by itself. There were other dances, however, at which the intellectuals and the smart, fast set mingled to an extent which never happened at dinners or small social gatherings of any kind.

The Charity Ball, arranged annually for Christmas week by a group of socially prominent women, was open to any one who paid admission. As the laudable purpose of the committee in charge was to raise money for certain public institutions, and as the music provided was invariably excellent, this assembly drew members from every set; even certain individuals from the Brooklyn group were induced to leave their comfortable early Victorian houses on this occasion. A careful spectator might have noted, however, even though no lines were drawn at the box-office, that persons belonging to one caste seldom danced with persons belonging to another, while social distinctions of a decidedly marked character were observed by several of the boxholders, a number of whom never appeared on the floor at all.

It was after midnight when Mary and Byron joined the throng, stepping at once on to the waxed floor to sway to the rhythm of Sweet and Low Down, played with ecstatic fervour by Fletcher Henderson's band. During their first round of the hall Mary was kept continuously bowing to acquaintances. It seemed to her that she had never before encountered so many of her friends at one party. In a box, surrounded by a laughing company, sat Adora in a dress of black sequins, a red poppy at her belt. Mrs. Albright occupied another box alone; Hester, for the moment, was not visible. Dr. Lister was dancing with his wife. Sergia Sawyer, as she circled the hall, stared at the crowd over Irwin Latrobe's shoulder. What a lot of gossip she would be prepared to disseminate on the morrow! thought Mary. Dick Sill was dancing with an unknown blonde in raspberry velvet, so light in complexion and yet so typically Negroid in her movements that it was impossible to be sure whether she were white or coloured. Carmen Fisher, in cloth of gold embroidered with pearls, clasped her brown arms languidly around the shoulders of Guymon Hooker. Galva Waldeck, in a Velázquez dress of orange taffeta embellished with wide bands of lace, was dancing with Léon Cazique. Mary began to wonder if this were a romance. She caught a glimpse of Sylvia Hawthorne, looking very tired, dancing with her husband. Rumsey Meadows, for once, was not in evidence. She saw Ray and Wren Hurley; she knew they must have motored in from New Jersey, where, fifty miles in the country, he was president of a small college. Montrose Esbon, who lived in Greenwich Village, wove his intricate way skilfully in and out of the dancers, holding Yuma Niland in his arms. Mimi Daquin, the pretty Creole, with her oval, cream-coloured face and her reddish-gold hair set off by her frock of absinthe-green, followed the music with Weston Underwood. . . . And there were hundreds more.

From the centre of the ceiling depended a huge, closed, silver bell which reflected the constantly shifting hues dispatched in broad shafts of light from calcium lamps in the corners of the hall. These lights tinged the gold and bronze in the rich brocaded dresses. Silver and copper glittered, satin and velvet shone, under the ministrations of this unnatural illumination. Mary, as always, was fascinated by the variations in colour in the faces of the men, the shoulders of the women: black shoulders, brown shoulders, tan shoulders, ivory shoulders.

As the music stopped—they had been dancing the second and last encore—the hall blazed in a brilliant white light. Mary became aware of the presence of many more acquaintances. She bowed to Mrs. Sumner and Campaspe Lorillard, sitting side by side in a box. She also found herself facing Hester Albright, whom she had not previously encountered, as usual accompanied by Orville Snodes. She introduced the pair to Byron.

What a pretty party! Hester breathed ecstatically. Everybody looks so well!

Mary could not avoid observing that Hester was wearing a gown of black and yellow striped satin, cut princesse, with very long, tight sleeves and a train. On another this robe might have appeared picturesque. Hester merely succeeded in looking more dowdy than usual.

Très, très jolie, Orville echoed in his thin, squeaky voice. What charming music! Charmante!

It makes you dance, Byron commented dryly.

Of course, the crowd is pretty vulgar. That notorious Sartoris woman is here, right after that dreadful scandal with Sid Hawthorne too.

I didn't know that there was a dreadful scandal, Mary remarked quietly.

Why, Sergia Sawyer . . .

Well, of course . . . Where is Mrs. Sartoris? Mary demanded.

I don't see her now. She is in red, a loud shade of red.

Orange, Orville contradicted, with some daring, Mary thought.

Scarlet, snapped Hester. Bright scarlet. Why there, she exclaimed, is that awful Randolph Pettijohn. In Washington we never have mixed parties like this!

Mary was no longer listening. Instinctively she had turned to look for the Bolito King. As he bowed to her formally she returned his greeting. She wondered who could be the girl by his side. She was very pretty in her golden-brown way, but there was an air about her which suggested that she was not quite at home in this environment. Even her dress, rose crêpe georgette strewn with purple velvet orchids, was a trifle theatrical, and her white stockings and bronze-green shoes were in deplorable taste.

You are a newcomer in our midst? Mary heard Orville demand of Byron.

Yes, was Byron's laconic response.

Why, there's Adora Boniface! Hester shrilled. You know she's a former stage woman. People like that would never be received in Washington. Society is so mixed here.

How's your mama? Mary inquired, with a swift anxiety to change the subject. I saw her in a box a little while ago.

She's not very well, Hester replied. The weather's so nasty and it affects her rheumatism. Poor mama! She's been quite poorly.

Un peu malade, un petit peu, Orville explained. He rubbed his pale palms together and stared fixedly at Byron.

We just made her come tonight, she goes out so little, Hester continued. Do go and speak to her.

I shall, Mary promised, as she turned away.

Vulgar prig! Byron was in a bad temper.

Well, she can't help it, Mary said, but Orville is a little too much even for me.

Silly nance! Byron growled.

Dear old ruffian, when I dance with you I forget all of them.

Me too!

They're playing the Tin Roof Blues!

And we're dancing it! He clasped her in his arms. This time she buried her head shamelessly in his shoulder, and did not look up.

After the second encore they found themselves standing near Ollie and Howard.

Some swell affair! Olive cried. How's the young sheik?

How's la sheba? Byron retorted, smiling.

How's your old man or what have you? a new voice broke in.

Mary turned to face the good-humoured countenance of Montrose Esbon.

Hello, Monte! she cried. How did you get way up here?

All God's chillun's got a Ford! he explained.

Where's Yuma?

Sheiks are all after her. . . . He drew a safety razor blade from his waistcoat pocket. . . . They'd better look out. I'm big, bad Bill when I get started. I brought this along for carving. I don't let anybody two-time me!

I see her, said Olive, over there in that box.

My God! With the Garvey nobility, the Duchess of the Bronx and the Countess of Hackensack! If she travels with those dames I'll have to get a Packard! Or else, he turned to Olive, take you on in her place and commit moral turpitude.

Be yourself! Olive laughed.

> Lad, never dam your body's itch
> When loveliness is seen,

he quoted.

Look at Russia Cloudcroft, Howard interrupted. She has a brow like a thunderstorm.

The Harlem Hedda Gabler! Montrose described her.

She's the berries at that, was Olive's comment. Better undam your itches for *her,* Monte!

I'm too blue for that pink-chaser. She's just unsheiked her husband. He was too blue too. Well, he added, I'm off, as the jim crow flies!

Who was that? Byron inquired.

Montrose Esbon—teaches French in a High School. I keep forgetting that you don't know everybody.

He's an amusing fellow—not much like a teacher.

He doesn't unload his French on the dancing public, said Olive.

What did he mean by calling that girl the Harlem Hedda Gabler?

She's unhappy because she isn't white, Mary explained.

Unhappy! She's positively glum! Olive elaborated. Funny thing about those pink-chasers, the ofays never seem to have any use for them. Hey! Hey! Do that thing! Here's another tune!

Dance it with me, urged Byron.

Boy, I'm your willing victim. She slipped into his arms and they disappeared in the crowd.

Well, Mary, aren't you dancing with me? Howard demanded.

She stood for a moment confused. Somehow it hadn't occurred to her to make allowances for the fact that Byron would occasionally dance with some one besides her. Of course, she might have known that he would not dance *all* the dances with her. Still . . . She accepted Howard's proposal, although without much enthusiasm.

Somehow I don't feel like dancing, she said after they had made one round of the hall. Let's sit down, Howard.

They had stopped near Adora's box and that one, glass in hand, hailed her friend.

Come in, Mary! How are you?

They entered the box.

Guess you know everybody here. Have some tea! Adora passed Howard a silver flask.

Piqua, find another glass!

Mrs. St. Paris imperilled her mauve satin by kneeling to search under a chair.

You can have mine, Howard, Mary said.

And mine too? Howard demanded.

There's plenty, Adora asserted. Don't be mean to yourself!

Save some for me! cried the moon-faced Lutie Panola, pounding her heels on the floor.

You'd better bant, Lutie, suggested Dr. Lister.

Be your age, George! I'll never start banting at a party.

You'll never start then, was Arabia Scribner's comment. You haven't missed a party since you came out!

Came out where? shouted Lutie.

Sh! Adora adjured her.

Why aren't you dancing, Adora? Mary, who had

slipped into a vacant chair beside Mrs. Boniface, inquired.

Why aren't you? Same reason, I guess. Too much crowd. I need room. It's too hot to navigate around that floor. Have some tea. . . . Adora emptied her own glass.

No, thank you. I'm afraid that would make me hotter.

Adora adjusted her ermine wrap around her shoulders. It's positively cold if you sit still, she complained. There's a draught from that window and I get tired of asking somebody to close it. Did you see Rannie? she whispered to Mary.

Yes, I did.

He's got a nerve coming to a dance like this with that . . .

Who is she? Mary inquired.

She's a tart, Adora replied, a little street-walker named Ruby Silver. He's keeping her. Everybody knows that, but he don't have to trot her out as if she was a prize filly. You bet he won't bring her to my house.

Trot who out? demanded Alcester Parker who had just entered the box.

I'll trot you out, if you can't make yourself behave, Adora announced severely.

On the floor Mary could see Hester hopping about with Orville for all the world as though they were skipping rope. Olive and Byron she could not discover.

Mary looked behind her. Howard had disappeared. Lutie was singing a song which seemed to have no connection rhythmically or melodically with the music the band was playing. Piqua and Arabia hovered like guardian angels over their affluent friend.

Come on and dance, Mary, Dr. Lister invited.

Not just now, George, thank you. I have a headache. I think, Adora, I'll speak to one or two more people while I have the chance.

Come back later, urged Adora, as Mary left the box.

She walked down the aisle behind the row of boxes. On the railing of this row a strange, young man was attempting to dance the Charleston. At small tables, groups had gathered to drink and chatter. Their laughter rang high over the music. The band was still playing, but as she searched the floor again, she could see no trace of Byron and Ollie. I'll make him look me up, she said to herself, but she was trembling with agitation.

She extended her hand to Mrs. Sumner, sitting back in her cloak of sable, and then to Mrs. Lorillard, in orchid satin with a band of uncut turquoises around her throat and a cluster of scarlet geraniums at her waist.

I'm delighted to see you again, Miss Love, Campaspe greeted her. I *did* enjoy that exhibition of African sculpture. I've bought several pieces for myself since.

Sit down, Mary, please, Mrs. Sumner urged.

Mary sat down. *He* was nowhere in sight. Hester, hopping, bobbing, Russia Cloudcroft, how many more, had circled the floor twice, but she could not find him.

I suppose this is a novel experience for you, Mrs. Lorillard? She was trying to make herself agreeable.

Not precisely that, Campaspe averred, but a charming one.

You've been to coloured balls before?

No, never! I mean I've been to balls before. They're all more or less alike. The differences are in favour of this one. What beautiful women! What handsome men! What a fascinating kaleidoscope of colour! And what fervour! You know, Emily—she turned to Mrs. Sumner—I like people who live.

I know you do, Mrs. Sumner replied. How is Byron getting on? she asked Mary.

Fine, thank you, Mary responded.

Has he found something to do?

Oh yes, he's got something splendid! . . . The next instant she wondered what had made her utter this falsehood.

I'm delighted to hear it. Aaron had something in mind—something good too—which he thought might suit him, but Byron hasn't been near us.

He's been so busy, Mary heard herself say.

Isn't that Florence Mills? Mrs. Lorillard inquired.

Yes, Mrs. Sumner replied, adding, She's promised to sing later.

Mary wondered if Mrs. Sumner knew she had been lying. Probably. She had not pursued the subject. She had asked no more questions about Byron. How could she, Mary, retract this impulsive and silly reply? Perhaps this might be Byron's great opportunity. What had made her prevaricate? Pride? False pride, she assured herself bitterly.

Mrs. Sumner and Mrs. Lorillard were conversing. Mary listened listlessly, her heart beating furiously. The floor was more crowded than ever. The dancing, moreover, had become wilder. A few couples were undertaking to do the Charleston together. The heat was overpowering. Collars, flowers, and frocks were wilting. Mary looked at the sad little bouquet of white violets at her waist. Occasionally a rich, mellow laugh rose over the soft moaning of the saxophone. Adora had thrown aside her cloak and was standing, her regal figure, shining with sequins, dominating the hall. Mary continued anxiously to inspect the faces of the dancers. Suddenly, she caught a glimpse of Ollie, and Ollie was dancing with Howard!

Who is that? Mrs. Lorillard demanded. The woman in blue.

That's Lasca Sartoris, Mary heard Mrs. Sumner reply.

Mary stared ahead of her. There he was, dancing with that exotic Negro sense of rhythm which made time a thing in space. In his arms was the most striking woman Mary had ever seen. A robe of turquoise-blue satin clung to her exquisite body, brought out in relief every curve. The dress was cut so low in front that the little depression between her firm, round breasts was plainly visible. Her golden-brown back was entirely nude to the waist. The dress was circled with wide bands of green and black sequins, designed to resemble the fur of the leopard. A tiara of sapphires sparkled in her hair, and a choker of these stones, around her throat.

What an extraordinary woman! Mrs. Lorillard exclaimed. Like a cocotte of the golden era! I don't think I've ever heard her name before.

She lives in Paris, Mrs. Sumner was explaining. She's only been back a short time.

Mary, through a mist, saw Dick Sill approaching the box.

Won't you dance with me, Mary? he demanded.

It's so warm, she protested. Yes, I will, she contradicted herself at once.

I wish you'd come to see me, Miss Love, Mrs. Lorillard suggested: Perhaps Emily would bring you.

I'd adore to, Mary murmured, as she went away with Dick.

The heat was killing her. She had no desire to dance, but she put new lightness into her feet, flinging her whole body into the now detestable rhythm. When the music stopped she awarded the orchestra abandoned applause.

I've never known you to dance like this before, Sill assured her. I thought you said you were tired.

I never was less tired in my life.

Suddenly, near them rose a shriek. They turned to see two women, strangers, each pulling at the hair of the other.

I'll teach you to leave my man be! one was screaming.

Two men separated the combatants. The victim of the assault stood in an attitude of defiance, her arms akimbo. I ain't interested in your man, she taunted her assailant. I can't help it if he follows me wherever I go. I can't help it if he writes me notes every day and sends me flowers and candy. I can't help it, can I? I don't want your man, ain't got a bit o' use for him, but he's jes' nacherly bent on pursuin' . . . The music closed over the incident as the waves close over a ship wrecked in the middle of the ocean. The dancing crowd blotted out the spectacle. Gaiety and charm everywhere; gaiety and charm and rhythm.

Primitive! thought Mary, exulting. Savage!

Suddenly, quite by chance, a space cleared on the

floor and over it she watched Lasca and Byron glide, softly, dangerously, like panthers. In an instant they had disappeared.

Wilder! Wilder! she urged Dick.

What's the matter with you tonight, Mary? he inquired. You're like a flame.

All over the hall they were singing:

> Oh, how I'm aching for love!
> Wish I had a little turtle dove
> To coo, coo, coo to me . . .

When the music stopped Mary and Dick found themselves by the side of Byron and Lasca.

Been looking for you everywhere, Mary, Byron said. This is Mrs. Sartoris, Miss Love and Mr. Sill.

Oh, I know Lasca! Dick exclaimed.

Dick and I are old friends, she remarked, as she clasped his proffered hand.

Mary had not given her hand. She said, So you're the famous Mrs. Sartoris!

Infamous, you mean! Lasca tossed back her head and laughed.

Mary was silent. People shouldn't talk like that, she was thinking.

Lasca's a wonderful sport, Mary, Byron spoke with enthusiasm. Did you see us doing the Charleston together?

No, I didn't, she replied. So he called her Lasca! She recalled that it was not till their third meeting that he had called her Mary. She could hear him demanding, Lasca, may I call you Mrs. Sartoris?

Well then, watch us in the next dance, Mrs. Sartoris invited.

Byron looked a trifle astonished, but also Mary could see that he was definitely pleased. She was certain from his expression that he had not asked the woman for the next dance. The perfect poise of this daring creature amazed Mary. Would he refuse?

Yes, she heard him say, watch us, Mary.

How Mary hated her! How she longed for the strength, the primitive impulse that would urge her to spring at Lasca's throat, tear away the collar of sapphires, disfigure that golden-brown countenance with her nails.

What about the one after that, Mary? Byron suggested.

It's taken, Mary retorted defiantly.

Then suppose you give me that one too, Lasca begged with her divine smile. You're really too generous, Miss Love. Byron is the best dancer here.

Even in her present mood, Mary could not fail to appreciate the rich music in the woman's voice, the grace of her carriage as she stood resting her weight on one foot while with the other she carelessly traced an invisible pattern on the floor. She also became aware of the flexible bands of diamonds on the woman's arms, the huge cabochon emeralds on her fingers. She tried to subdue her pride, to conquer her absurd feeling of jealousy—it must be absurd, she attempted to assure herself; why, Byron has only just met this woman—to withdraw her refusal, when the music started and he and Lasca were swept away in the maelstrom of dancers.

Some sheba, Lasca! Dick commented. Whew! She'll make a dent in Harlem.

Mary was silent. In vain her eyes sought out the departed pair.

Shall we dance, Mary?

Dick, I've got a headache. Please take me to the dressing-room.

Presently she found herself alone in the room—even the maid in attendance had disappeared for the moment. Staring at her image in the mirror, she was not reassured by what she saw.

I can't do it, she moaned. I ought to kill her, I want to, but I can't. What's wrong with me?

She sank into a chair and gave way to an uncontrollable fit of sobbing.

BOOK TWO

BYRON

One

Byron read the letter he had just received from his father.

My dear boy, it began:

I do not want to appear unsympathetic, but the fact remains that you have been in New York more than two months without making any place for yourself. When you informed me that you wished to undertake a writer's career, I gave you what encouragement I could, at the same time laying before you the reasons why, as a coloured man, you would have difficulty in carrying out that project. I also told you that you would have to support yourself, as I feel I have done all I can afford to do for you in sending you through college.

We need not go into the reasons for your leaving Philadelphia. We both agreed, in the circumstances, that this would be a wise move. You, quite naturally, chose Harlem as the alternative. Harlem is a great Negro city, the greatest Negro city in the world, and it is surely as full of pitfalls for young men as all great cities are. Unavoidably you will encounter your share of temptations. You are to an unfortunate extent, as we know to our cost, a slave to your appetites. Furthermore you are inclined to be headstrong and obstinate, and sensitive to an abnormal degree. I am being very frank with you now, because you must be aware that no one more than I do appreciates your good qualities, the foremost of which in my opinion is your race pride.

I am mentioning these things because I hear from Aaron Sumner that you have not presented yourself to him since the day you first brought him my letter of introduction. I hear from others that you have not presented my letters at all. I know how your touchiness inclines to make you feel any demonstration of sympathy from others as patronizing. Naturally, therefore, I feel some anxiety on your account.

The late Booker T. Washington preached industry and thrift. He in his wisdom realized that the advancement of the Negro would come only through economic progress. I have always felt in this regard that it is no disgrace for us to accept what labour is given us to perform in the spirit in which it is offered. If you are a natural born writer you will eventually write, no matter what else you may be compelled to do in the meantime. Indeed, whatever struggles you may be obliged to undergo will only add to your desire to write, if you cherish a sincere desire. My advice to you, therefore, is to seek honest employment. If your colour prevents you from securing a clerkship, accept a job as a porter or an elevator boy. Your education has unfitted you for such humble pursuits, but your colour, temporarily, may bar your advancement in other directions. When you have proved that you have literary ability and can sell your stories, I shall be the first to recognize that fact and to encourage you to go farther. Bear in mind that Paul Laurence Dunbar wrote the poems which brought him recognition while *he* was an elevator boy.

In the meantime, I feel that it would be doing you a wrong

if I continued to send you money. With the small amounts I can afford to give you you certainly would not be able to live a life of luxury, but you could live a life of idleness so that it would be a simple matter for you to fall into bad habits and evil ways. The cheque I am enclosing in this letter, therefore, is the last I shall send.

It has been very difficult for me to write this letter, but I know the weaknesses in your nature. It is for you to rise superior to these, and if you are a real man you will do so. Always, my dear boy, you have my love and that of your mother.

Raising his eyes from the last lines of this letter, Byron stared hopelessly out of his little window. Only a blank wall rewarded his vision, a wall erected so near the window that even on bright days he could only see to read by the aid of a gas-jet. His soul was full of resentment, the more so because he recognized the justice of his father's words, the calm of his epistolary tone: a maddening, judicial calm. It's bad enough to know all this without having it rubbed in, he muttered to himself. His mind reverted to the sordid episode at which his father had tactfully hinted. There had been an unfortunate affair with a servant-girl at college, but his father had never heard of that or of many other adventures of which he had been the sorry hero. The incident to which his father referred had occurred only last summer in Philadelphia. He had become involved in an affair with a married woman, an affair of which the woman's husband had become cognizant. It was only because the husband desired above all else to avoid a scandal that he, Byron, had been let off so easily. Even so, it was stipulated that he should leave Philadelphia. His friends had wondered why he had not returned for the great Howard-Lincoln football game at Thanksgiving, why he had not visited his family at Christmas. . . . He looked at the cheque again and laughed. Twenty-five dollars wouldn't last very long. . . . God! he moaned, I've tried hard enough to find work. His memory reviewed all the advertisements he had answered, the humiliations he had endured, the long series of refusals, couched in insulting terms, that he had encountered. He could scarcely tolerate the idea of making renewed efforts in this direction. Yet, he realized, he had so far only attempted to secure positions offered to college men, only open, the event proved, to *white* college men. He had not yet descended to asking for what his father so nobly termed honest employment. He felt that he would almost rather starve first. By God, if his education were worth nothing to him why had he taken the trouble to get a college degree? A Negro with a college degree is two steps ahead of his uneducated brothers, every one had assured him, and his attention was directed to the number of graduates who had risen to such heights in their race that they lived lives of comparative ease and comfort, respected even by white people. Yes, there was plenty of that sort of thing around him. Why was it so difficult for him to make a start?

His room was so small that it was almost possible for him to touch every article of furniture without moving from his chair at his writing-table. Often, when he was trying to write, he spread his books of reference open on his bed. He could reach for matches on the adjacent bureau. He turned to this bureau now and from one of the drawers extracted a pile of manuscript, written in pencil.

Was he a writer? he wondered. Was there any excuse for him to go ahead, for him to continue to fill up these sheets of paper with these foolish hieroglyphics? So many stories he had begun and so many he had found it impossible to round out. He glanced swiftly over some of the pages. The stories all started out well enough, he told himself. He possessed a gift—his instructors at Pennsylvania had assured him of that—for delineating character in action, for swift description, occasionally for dialogue, but apparently he had no sense of construction. Somewhere along towards the middle, his stories fell apart. They were spineless. The worst difficulty of all was to find a subject: there was so little to write about.

Try as he might, he could not get away from propaganda. The Negro problem seemed to hover over him and occasionally, like the great, black bird it was, claw at his heart. In his stories this influence invariably made itself felt, and it was, he was sometimes convinced, the very thing that kept him from doing better work. Wheels within wheels. A vicious circle.

Could he overcome this obstacle? Unwillingly he was obliged to acknowledge to himself that certain writers of his race had overcome it, particularly Charles Waddell Chesnutt, an author strangely unfamiliar to most of the new generation. Byron himself, indeed, had been introduced to his books by a white professor at college. He lifted The Wife of his Youth from its place on his table and opened its pages for the hundredth time. How much he admired the cool deliberation of its style, the sense of form, but more than all the civilized mind of this man who had surveyed the problems of his race from an Olympian height and had turned them into living and artistic drama. Nothing seemed to have escaped his attention, from the lowly life of the worker on the Southern plantation to the snobbery of the near whites of the North. Chesnutt had surveyed the entire field, calmly setting down what he saw, what he thought and felt about it.

Byron especially admired the story called A Matter of Principle which related the painful experience of the Clayton family, members of the Blue Vein Circle in a middle western city. At a dance in Washington, the daughter, Alice, met a number of attractive young men. Shortly after her return to her home she received a note from a coloured Congressman informing her that he would soon be paying a visit to her city and begging to be permitted to call. The letter was couched in terms that indicated beyond any manner of doubt that the Congressman was deeply interested in Alice. She, however, had danced with so many young men that she was unable to recall this particular one. As a Congressman he assuredly had some political importance. The paramount question with her family, belonging as it did to the Blue Veins, was whether he was sufficiently light in colour to be received by their group. Local inquiry elicited a favourable report. The Congressman, therefore, was invited to stop at Mr. Clayton's house and a reception was arranged in his honour. At the appointed hour Mr. Clayton and his son repaired to the railway station to meet him. Somehow they missed him at the gate. Searching the waiting-rooms they came upon a bag which was plainly marked with their prospective guest's initials, but what was their chagrin to discover standing next to the bag an extremely black man. They receded to confer. Obviously their set would laugh if they went through with their plan to entertain this fellow. In their desperation they remembered that an epidemic of diphtheria was raging in the city. Hastily scribbling a note of apology—it described Alice as laid low with the disease—they dispatched it by a porter to the owner of the bag. Alice subsequently was required to take to her bed, the invitations to the reception were cancelled by telephone, and a friendly physician was bribed to add a quarantine sign to the decorations of the front porch. These precautionary measures attended to, the family breathed a sigh of relief wh'ch was transformed, the next morning, into a groan, when they read in the local newspaper a long interview with the Congressman, who was described as nearly white. Thereafter for the week he remained in town they read accounts of the entertainments given for him by the Blue Veins while Alice was compelled to remain in bed. The dark stranger in the station, it appeared, was a bishop who had been the Congressman's travelling companion.

Byron knew in his soul that this story explained why he had not taken advantage of Mr. Sumner's offer to help him secure a position, why he had not called on several other prominent men to whom his father had given him letters. It might be unfair—it probably was—but he felt that these people were snobs and he did not want to be beholden to them. In fact, something stronger than himself, a kind of perverse pride, refused to permit him to make any use of such acquaintanceships. These successful persons liked to be seen with whites or with the light coloured or more famous members of their own race. Well, until he was famous he refused to be patronized.

What a great man Chesnutt must have been to dare publish A Matter of Principle in 1900, before there were any "New Negroes!" Why now, all the young writers who were trying to set down on paper what they knew to be true were branded by the uncultured mob as faithless to their race, untrue to their trust. Their trust! Byron flamed as he thought how the uneducated Negroes delighted in keeping the upper level as low as possible, pulling them down, maliciously, even with glee, when they were able to do so.

His mind travelled irrationally to a consideration of Lasca Sartoris, a pleasanter subject which brought a smile and a cigarette simultaneously to his lips. She had beauty and wit and money. She was rich and successful and happy. She had won. Problems didn't bother her. She had found what she had wanted by wanting what she could get, and then always demanding more, more, until now the world poured its gifts into her bewitching lap. But Lasca Sartoris was a woman, and an exceptionally fascinating woman. Men gave *her* things, but who would give him anything? Lasca Sartoris! If he might only know her better! *That* would give him something! Never before had he met so vibrant a personality . . . and golden-brown, his colour.

Mary's behaviour at the dance had surprised him. Somehow he hadn't foreseen that she would be jealous. He had been attracted initially by the cool simplicity of her manner. She had been so different from most of the women he had known. . . . Arline, little spitfire! . . . Immediately he had met Mary, he was aware that he made subtle distinctions in her favour, had even acknowledged to himself that she had a certain power over him, and yet he had not exactly intended to become engaged to her. He loved Mary now that he had awakened an unsuspected fire in her, but he knew that this was a very different Mary from the Mary that had first attracted his attention at Adora's: a passionate, jealous Mary with an unpleasant sense of possession. He would, he was sure, constantly strive to escape from this. He was doomed to hurt her. She frightened him; her hurt frightened him. Why, he had to know women like Lasca! He could never resist women anyway—golden-brown women; Mary, too, was golden-brown—and a woman like Lasca drew him inevitably to her side. He hadn't, however, seen her again. He had telephoned her twice, only to be mysteriously informed that she was out of the city. He didn't actually want to leave Mary, he tried to tell himself—God knows Lasca, with everything she desired within reach, wouldn't take him very seriously—but he had to teach her that she didn't own him.

There was still another way in which Mary irked him, another direction in which she exercised her sense of possession. Like his father, she was for ever offering him advice, telling him what he must do to get on. These two didn't seem to realize what getting on meant. It had been comparatively easy for Mary, easy enough, no doubt, even for his father. They couldn't understand how hard it had been for him. They couldn't understand that he had tried. Had he tried? His mind began to wander. What was it all worth, anyway? Why couldn't he fall in line and just be a Nigger, like the rest of the "good" Niggers! . . . And Mary didn't like cabarets and would be disagreeable every time he went to one, and she would be annoyed if he attended prize-fights—he made a mental note that he would see Leanshanks Pescod's next combat . . . and girls, golden-brown girls. What would Mary . . . ?

His landlady rapped on the door. Welcome Fox was a middle-aged woman who had been born on a Tennessee plantation and had come North with her husband, at that time working as a coachman for a family which had moved to New York. He had, in time, drifted away from this connection to drive one of the Victorias that rolled in the old days up and down Fifth Avenue. Two years ago he had died, leaving his wife to care for their dead daughter's two children. Mrs. Fox had always been thrifty, however, and she was accustomed to hard work. In her earlier days she had added to her income by taking in washing and doing simple dressmaking. Now she paid the rent of her apartment by letting some of the rooms. Occasionally, too, she worked out by the day. When she was at home she practically lived in the kitchen, although she also reserved a small bedroom for herself and the children.

Come in! Byron cried.

As Mrs. Fox opened the door, whiffs of frying pork-chops and boiled cabbage floated into the room. One of the children clung with a sort of desperation to her ample skirts.

Dere's a gen'mun ter see you, chile, she announced.

Who is it, Mrs. Fox?

Ah doan perzackly recerlec' duh name. It's duh light-coloured gen'mun who comes here frequent-like.

Mr. Sill?

Dat's him. Her pleasant face brightened. Taxis, quit pullin' yo' mammy's skirts. Ah declare dat chil' ain' nebber gwine leab me alone.

Before Dick Sill had removed his overcoat, he blazed forth his news, almost in a tone of defiance.

I'm going white! he announced.

Byron did not speak at once. He didn't know what to say. Presently, he mustered up, Take off your coat, Dick.

Accepting this invitation, his friend seated himself on the bed and nervously lighted a cigarette.

They make us do it, Byron, he insisted, still in an aggressive tone which sounded apologetic. They make us. We don't want to. *I* don't want to, but they make us.

I know, said Byron. I couldn't do it, but I know.

Buda Green married a white man. That's what got me to thinking. He doesn't know she has coloured blood. I met her on the street one day. Why don't you pass, too, Dick? she asked me. There are ten thousand of us in New York alone. Why don't you come across the line? You're light enough.

Suppose somebody'd give me away, I countered. She laughed at me. They won't do that, she said. Shines love to fool ofays too much for that and when they see you fooling 'em they'll leave you alone. *They* won't blab on you. You're a boob if you don't come over. Why, I go everywhere with my husband and no one has ever suspected me. Why should they? The world is full of mixed blood, Chinese and English, Indians and American whites, Jews and Spaniards . . .

I read somewhere, said Byron, about a fellow who holds a theory that this . . . this . . . flair the white man has for our women will eventually solve the race problem. We'll all be absorbed in the white race!

Say, I've read a thing or two on the subject myself, cried Dick, still more excitedly. The other day I ran across a book by an English chap named Robert Graves. It's called My Head! My Head!

I opened it to these words: There were only two women who loved Moses, and no men. The women were Jochebed, his mother, and the Ethiopian woman, his wife. . . . Say, that startled me and I went back and read from the beginning. I found the book to be a loving, skilful interpretation of the story of Moses, as related by Elisha to the Shunamite woman who was the namesake of Moses's mother. The book explains that it was through the aid of the Ethiopian woman, born near the springs of the Nile, that Moses was enabled to predict the plagues of Egypt, partly through her knowledge of voodoo, partly through advance information she secured from her tribe.

But that's fiction! It isn't in the Bible! Byron cried.

Isn't it just? Well, the first verse of the twelfth chapter of Numbers reads: And Miriam and Aaron spoke against Moses because of the Ethiopian woman whom he married; for he had married an Ethiopian woman. . . . And because Miriam and Aaron objected to her, Dick continued, the Bible tells us that God turned them into lepers. That'll be news for some of these Southern fundamentalists. Apparently there's nothing against miscegenation in Holy Writ. What's more, I looked the lady up in Josephus, and found her there, too, together with her name, Tharbis.

And so you think . . . ?

I think that anything Moses did in Egypt a great many of his followers did too. I think . . .

Surely you're not passing because you've been reading the Bible!

Not at all! It just happened accidentally. You know I recently lost my job. Well, I was searching another. Want-ad-page in hand, I hustled from office to office. Always turned down when I told them I was a Negro. Finally, I went into an office where they were very pleasant to me and the job looked fine. After the man asked me several questions, he engaged me. Then he inquired, You're quite dark. Are you Spanish?

My mother was Spanish, I replied. Do you blame me?

No, I don't, Byron assured him. I couldn't. What kind of job is it?

I'm private secretary. The boss makes frequent trips to Europe. We're sailing, as a matter of fact, in April.

Byron buried his face in his hands and groaned. I don't blame you, Dick, he replied, but I just couldn't do it myself.

A little later, after his friend had departed, Byron drew out a fresh sheet of paper and took up his pencil. He looked out of the window at the blank wall and tried to collect his thoughts. What could he write about? What was there interesting to write about? He couldn't think of a thing.

Two

Unaccustomed to early rising, Byron had found it practical to purchase an alarm-clock which he had set for six o'clock. When, at the hour appointed, the angry bell jangled in his ears, he turned over and yawned, stretching his arms. Then he tried to doze, but the horrid tocsin still sounded. At last remembering that he had accepted a job in the city and had been ordered to appear at seven-thirty, he forced himself to get out of bed. The room was quite dark and on his way to the gas-burner, he stumbled over a pile of books he had left on the floor. After he had ignited the gas he sponged himself perfunctorily. The touch of the cold water to his flesh, however, revivified him sufficiently to enable him to dress rapidly. He had requested Mrs. Fox to leave the coffee-pot prepared on the stove so that he soon made a steaming cup of coffee. That, together with a couple of slices of bread he had cut and buttered, constituted his breakfast. To his astonishment he discovered that he was not in low spirits. On the contrary, he felt excited. Young and healthy as he was, he was looking forward to the day's work in the light of an adventure.

When, at seven, he emerged from the house, it

was beginning to grow lighter, although the sky was shrouded with clouds. Sporadically, he was conscious that a drop of rain beat against his cheek. As he walked briskly towards the nearest elevated station, he fell into what seemed to be an endless procession. The journalistic phrase, two hours passing the grandstand, came into his mind. From all the side-streets, up the avenues, they marched: Negro workmen and working-women, all leaving the walled, black city temporarily to labour in an alien world. Some were bowed and old and walked slowly and with pain. Others were young and sinewy and chattered as they marched rapidly forward. The thought struck him that it was like a symbolic procession, the procession of an oppressed people. Thus the Jews went out into the desert to build pyramids for the Pharaohs. Thus, under the knout, the Russian political prisoners plodded to Siberia. Only, and Byron was quick to sense the distinction, from the eyes of all these people around him peered an expression of hope. They were doing what they had to do before the millennium, the day when the black race would be on a level with the white. It was coming; they all felt that, although the old and the helpless feared they would never live to see it.

Dere's fire in duh East;
Dere's fire in duh West;
Oh, send dem angels down!

There was more than hope in these eyes: Byron noted the generally gay insouciance, the careless, carefree manner of these servant-girls, these stevedores and messenger boys. They had a life and independence of their own, that no amount of hardship could take from them. On the whole they were happier, he was sure, than white servant-girls ever could be, doomed, as they were, to drudgery from early morning until they went to bed late at night. Every evening these race sisters of his returned to their families, to their daddies; they refused to "live in." The white world might do its best to rob their days of pleasure, but they could always look forward to the evening.

Byron passed a cabaret that was just closing. Out of the sleepy, yawning jaw of the dive, they came, these young men and women who had been dancing the night through. They, too, joined the procession. They had had no sleep. After a night devoted to gaiety they were returning to take their places as pawns in this strange game of toil that the white world insisted upon playing.

We should all of us be singing, Byron thought, and he wondered what would be appropriate. Onward, Christian Soldiers? Smiling, he rejected Sullivan's hymn. Something of our own: perhaps Walk together, children! Only, he added to himself, we so seldom do walk together in spirit.

Byron had never lived in or visited the South and therefore had never seen a Jim Crow car in his life, but the moving car, in which he was presently standing, must be very much like one, he thought. The procession had crowded into it, together with the other cars that made up the train, although all the seats had already been pre-empted by black workers who had entered at stations further up the line. There were, to be sure, a few white faces, faces of men and women who had come from the upper reaches of the island, but most of the skins were black or brown or mulatto. We should be known as the rainbow race, Byron assured himself.

He marvelled as he reflected that he was bound to a destination similar to that which was the goal of all these others, and yet he was not acquainted with a single person in the car. Perhaps even, he mused, their whole thinking processes, their very ideas, are different. I am no more like them than they are like me, than I am like any of my friends, he assured himself. In temperament and opinions we all disagree. Each of us has his own standard of thought and behaviour and yet we are forced by this prodigious power of prejudice to line up together. To the white world we are a mass. . . .

What would happen to this mass? Might it not be possible that prejudice was gradually creating, automatically and unconsciously, a force that would eventually solidify, in outward opinion at least, a mass that might even assume an aggressive attitude? Or would this mass, under this pressure of prejudice, be dissipated and swept apart?

There was Dick. That was one solution, an easy, pleasant solution for people of Dick's complexion, and what Dick had done hundreds had done before him and thousands would do after him. Byron reflected that during the period he had spent in New York he had encountered more and more coloured people who were nearly white. Would the race eventually lose its identity? Was it destined to dissolve in this white blood?

He considered another alternative. When a coloured family moved into an apartment, all the white families fled. When two coloured families moved into a block, the block was deserted by the white occupants. So Harlem, in its African aspects, had been created. So Harlem was slowly growing, east and west, north and south, growing, slowly growing. Might it not eventually happen, as more Negroes, coming from the South, coming from the West, to take advantage of the opportunities promised by this new metropolis, encroached farther and farther on white territory, that Manhattan, which already had been Indian, Dutch, English, and finally the melting-pot for every nation, become a Negro island? Byron chuckled aloud as the vision came to him of the last white inhabitant pushing off in a row boat from the Battery while the black flag flew over the Aquarium and from the roof of every skyscraper. Or would property values in Harlem increase so substantially that it would be practical to sell the land and migrate again? Or would it ever be possible for white and black to live peaceably, side by side, each offering his gifts, one to the other? That consummation, Byron admitted to himself, was not to be immediately hoped for.

Forty-second Street! the guard was shouting. Byron left the car.

The Cletheredge Building was a huge nest of offices towering to the sky in the early forties, its upper storeys resting on a series of graceful terraces. The effect of the front portal, guarded by elaborately carved, sinister, stone dragons, was sombre and portentous. As Byron entered he recalled the device Dante had blazoned over the gates of hell.

In a spacious underground room he discovered a group of young Negroes, laughing, chattering, smoking cigarettes, as they donned their uniforms. In one corner, three boys were shooting craps.

Pull duh chain! one of them cried. Dis heah is duh new boy.

Whah you from? another demanded. Later, Byron identified him as the Joel to whom, the day before, he had been instructed to report.

Harlem, Byron replied.

Ah ain' seen you. Joel regarded the newcomer with suspicion.

Shoot duh fo'! a voice in the corner called.

Stop rollin' dose bones! Joel ordered. Then to Byron, Roll duh babies?

Sometimes.

Well, come along an' git yo' suit. Joel conducted

Byron to a locker. Dis one jes' lately been worn by a jig dat's fired. You better lock yo' clothes up. Heah's duh key. Ah can' 'count fo' duh actions an' movements o' dis bunch o' smokes.

As Byron on his bench began to pull off his trousers, the boys on the adjoining benches babbled on. They spoke freely about their amorous adventures, about games of craps, about dives on Lenox Avenue, about Numbers. He listened to accounts of the prowess of Tiger Flowers, of Leanshanks Pescod. To Byron the atmosphere was vaguely distasteful. You want to be a writer, he adjured himself, and this is probably first-class material. Nevertheless, his immediate pendent thought was that he would never write about this life, that he could never feel anything but repugnance for these people, because they were black. I can't bear to think of myself as a part of this, he sighed, and they . . .

Well, presently he knew what *they* thought. As a couple whispered, they gave sly nods in his direction; they laughed and winked. Soon, they carelessly raised their voices. He caught phrases: posin' an' signifyin', high-toned mustard-seed, arnchy yaller boy, sheik from Strivers' Row . . . Joel rescued him.

Come along, he commanded.

Byron, in his ill-fitting uniform of navy blue, embellished with brass buttons, obeyed. Joel led him to one of the elevators and explained to him how to adjust the lever.

Jump in an' ride wid me, he continued. Ah'll show you.

The morning ingress had begun. Brokers, lawyers, stenographers, office boys, were arriving in troops. Byron was amazed to observe the skill with which Joel operated the car, ready with a cheery good-morning for everybody that greeted him, while he slammed the iron gate back and forth at each landing, guiding the car dexterously to an exact level with each floor. All these manœuvres Byron, of course, had seen performed before, but with no comprehension of the difficulties they involved. Occasionally, as the hours wore on, the car would be deserted for a floor or two, and then Joel would permit the novice to manipulate the mechanism himself. Try as he might, however, Byron never seemed to be able to bring the elevator to a level with the landing. He began to regard Joel with a sneaking admiration.

At twelve o'clock Joel suggested, You better go an' git yo' lunch.

Where? Byron inquired. He was bewildered. He knew nothing about the restaurants in the neighbourhood. One might be too expensive; at another they might not admit a Negro.

Didn't you fetch none?

No, Byron replied. I didn't know. . . .

Well, Ah guess one o' duh boys'll give you a bite.

Joel dropped him off at the basement floor.

That night as usual Byron called on Mary. He wondered, now that he was working downtown, how he could manage to keep this up and do a little writing also. He would have to plan his hours. Now that his father had stopped his allowance, his wages gave him barely enough money on which to exist. He would be compelled to eschew social recreations until he might succeed in selling a short story.

Well, Olive demanded, as Mary opened the door to let Byron enter, how's the labouring man? I'm going to give you a pail to carry your lunch in.

I forgot my lunch today, Byron laughed, and I had to eat out of one of the other fellow's buckets.

What kind are they? Olive inquired.

Oh, all right, I guess. You know. You work downtown.

They're different in different buildings, Olive persisted. What kind are these?

Oh, I guess I could put up with them, Byron responded, but they seem to think I'm putting on airs. My clothes or my English are too good. One of 'em called me an arnchy.

I forgot to warn you, said Howard. You ought to speak in dialect. These low-class smokes haven't any use for a fellow that puts on airs. You have to be a mixer.

Well, I seem to be all wrong, Byron remarked ruefully. I can't begin to speak dialect tomorrow.

You can in your next place, Howard suggested significantly.

My next place?

Don't mean maybe. You won't last long after this kind of start. They'll put the rollers under you.

The telephone bell tinkled.

Hello, said Olive, lifting the receiver to her ear. Yes, he's here. Just a moment, please. . . . She pressed her palm against the transmitter . . . Howard, she whispered, it's Mr. Pettijohn.

Hello. Howard was at the telephone. Is that you, Mr. Pettijohn? You want to see me? . . . When? . . . Right away? Well, I don't know about that. I've got a mighty important case on hand. I expect to go over it with my client tonight. . . . That so? . . . Well, I might put him off till ten o'clock and come to see you first. . . . Yes, I'll do that, Mr. Pettijohn. . . . Howard was speaking with decision. . . . At your house? All right, I'll be right around.

Replacing the receiver, he whirled about to face the room.

Hurray! he cried. Hurray! I've hooked Pettijohn at last. He's had a row with Mainwaring and fired him. Why, the King has more law business than any one else in Harlem!

Olive was screaming with laughter. Gee, how well you bluffed him, Howard! Got to meet another client! And the King a gambler, too!

How much are you going to make? was her next question.

I don't know. Enough for wedding bells, I hope. Howard was drawing on his coat. Perhaps we'll even buy a struggle-buggy.

I'm going with you, Olive cried as she raced to her bedroom. Where does he live? she called.

It isn't far. Hundred and twenty-seventh Street.

Olive had returned with her cloak. I'll walk down with you, she said. I need the air. Besides, she added, I think I'll wait on the kerb till you come out. I've got to be the first to hear the big news.

The pair swung out of the room.

Byron stared at Mary. Pretty soft for Howard, he remarked bitterly. Pretty soft.

Mary tried to console him. I'm sorry that it isn't you, dear, she said, but remember that Howard's worked years for this. Think of all the time he spent in law school, and he's been out nearly a year without getting an important case.

Pretty slow, Byron groaned. He was standing now. To go from college directly to an elevator! I guess that'll lift me all right!

Don't! she begged him, raising his hand to her lips, Please don't!

Byron, she went on, I don't like this job of yours.

What else can I do?

We've got to find something. I know you've tried hard enough, but the whole world can't be prejudiced. Mr. Sumner said . . .

That snob! I don't want any of his help!

Byron!

I mean it. They've never asked me to their place since that night I met you there.

But why should they ask you, Byron?

They don't pay any attention to me. I suppose I'm not good enough for them.

Don't be silly. Mr. Sumner is far from being a snob. How can you expect him to find time to see everybody he knows? He's a very busy man, Byron, and you are probably one of a thousand young men who need his help. Do you expect him to be nice to them all? Be reasonable. It's your place to look *him* up.

Never. . . . He knows my father, he added lamely.

He knows mine too. Father stopped there the last time he was in town, but I don't ever expect to be invited there more than twice a year. They have too many obligations to be constantly attentive to everybody. You mustn't be so sensitive, she pleaded, rubbing his palm against her cheek. I've seen so many awful things happen through sensitiveness. Why, Mr. Sumner isn't even thinking about you. He's probably forgotten your very existence, and you believe he's consciously snubbing you. If you went to see him I'm sure he'd be delighted.

Roughly withdrawing his hand, Byron stalked across the floor. You don't give a damn about me yourself or you wouldn't be defending him! he cried, exasperated.

Byron, you ought to know how much I love you. I don't have to prove that, do I?

Funny kind of love! Always explaining to me why I ought to let somebody insult me! You don't talk to Howard this way, I notice.

I'm perhaps a little more interested in you than I am in Howard, she flamed, adding, Besides Howard doesn't need advice.

Oh, Howard's perfect, I suppose! I don't give a damn how interested you are in me if you always take somebody else's part.

I'll take yours when you deserve it. You're wrong about Mr. Sumner. You're behaving in a very silly manner and I'm going to tell you so whether you like it or not.

Fine way to spend an evening, Byron shouted. After working hard all day I come here when I ought to be home writing, and all I get is abuse.

I haven't noticed that you did so much writing before you took this job.

I haven't had a chance. You know I've been looking for work all the time.

Never play pool, do you? Or go to the Commonwealth Club? Or call on Mrs. Sartoris?

None of your God damn business what I do! Catching up his coat and hat, he flung the door open, and rushing out, slammed it behind him. As he raced down the hallway, he could hear her call out his name despairingly, but he did not turn back.

Three

Byron discovered that Howard had made a correct prognostication. Notwithstanding the fact that he soon found it possible to handle an elevator with almost as much skill as his instructor, at the end of the week he lost his job. Probably Joel had told the superintendent that he wouldn't do. Again began the weary round of employment agencies and office buildings. Again he was forced to endure bitter humiliation, although Byron vaguely realized that this humiliation was largely a matter of his own imagination, stimulated by his touchiness. Moreover his heart, never completely engaged, was no longer in the business, more especially because his father had been kind enough to send him another cheque—for a higher amount this time—without a word of advice or complaint.

He wished that he might look for as much understanding from Mary. It seemed impossible for them to meet without quarrelling. After several of these disagreements he was aware to some degree that what had happened was more his fault than hers. He was, in many ways, devoted to Mary, but she had become too critical of his actions, too demanding. Why couldn't she understand that a fellow had to grow? Cool reflection often informed him that she did, that she was trying her best to be fair, but when he was with her he resented this attitude more than anything else. How dare she try to be fair? He was enraged by this patronage, this condescension, as it seemed to him.

Sooner or later his thoughts obstinately reverted to Lasca. *She* had understanding. She, he felt certain, would give him sympathy. She was a real man's woman. He telephoned her more than once, but invariably received the message that she was still out of town and it was not known when she would return.

To rid himself of his recurring fits of depression, it became his habit to visit a pool-room where he could be sure of meeting fellows who were glad to see him, especially if he could pay for a drink. They often would go on to a cabaret to sit and talk or dance until late in the morning and it would be afternoon before he had summoned enough energy to start out on a renewed quest of employment.

Naturally his writing lagged. Sometimes he would sit before his table for an hour, striving to string words together. Nothing would come of this effort. His mind, he believed, was in too much of a turmoil, life disturbed him too much, to permit calm thinking and calm thinking was essential to a writer; he knew that. Further, there was the fundamental and disturbing question of a suitable subject. He seemed unable to assemble his material neatly, to select it. At college it had been different. There he had not tried to create fiction. He had written about plays he had seen in the theatre, incidents he had observed in the street. Here he saw too much, too much and too little. The habits of these people were both too familiar and too annoying to him. He loathed his landlady and her grandchildren. They were so good-hearted and so sordid. He had hated his working companions at the Cletheredge Building. They reminded him too painfully of his birthright. More than the others he detested the young Negro writers who were making names for themselves. Mary often pleaded with him to see more of them, but he always sullenly refused. He could not bear to think that they were getting on while he was still struggling at the foot of the ladder.

Unexpectedly one night, however, the scheme of a story came to him quite spontaneously—it had been suggested by an item in a newspaper. Elated, he immediately rushed to Mary to tell her the news. When he greeted her he was out of breath from running upstairs.

Whatever is the matter, Byron? she demanded, after she had kissed him.

I've got a wonderful idea for a story, Mary! he announced, puffing.

That's fine, dearest. Tell me about it.

He sat down to consider. The details were not

yet clear in his mind, although the main outline was there.

You see, he began, I'll have a white boy who frequents Harlem cabarets pick up a coloured girl and have an affair with her. He goes to see her all the time. Then, you see, this boy has a sister who works in a settlement house. One day she meets an intelligent, young coloured man engaged in the same work. They become interested in each other and eventually decide to marry. You see, they love one another . . . Byron hesitated.

Well? Mary inquired.

Don't you know what would happen? The white boy had regarded such relations on a different plane. He didn't mind seducing a coloured girl. The fact that she loved him didn't affect his point of view. It was just fun, not to be taken seriously. But his sister's desire was different. The idea that his sister could bring herself to marry a coloured fellow, even though he is educated and they love each other, is so horrible to him that he shoots his sister's fiancé.

There was silence for a moment.

It isn't just the sort of thing I expected you to write, Byron dear, Mary remarked presently, but go ahead with it and see what you can do.

What do you mean by saying it's not the sort of thing you expected me to write? He flared up at once.

Don't get excited, Byron. . . . She still hesitated. At last she went on diffidently, These propaganda subjects are very difficult, Byron, difficult, that is, to make human. It is hard to keep them from becoming melodramatic, cheap even. Unless such a story is written with an exquisite skill, it will read like a meretricious appeal to the emotions arising out of race prejudice.

And you don't think *I* can do it! Byron was furious.

I didn't say that, dearest. I didn't say that at all. I don't know whether you can do it or not, but I think it would be safer if you wrote about something you know more about.

Don't you think I know anything about this? I've just told you the story, haven't I?

It isn't the story that counts; it's the treatment. . . . Mary was speaking very softly. . . . Of course, you'll understand the psychology of the intelligent coloured man, but as you have related the story, he would be one of the least important characters. In a way, too, I suppose you'd get the coloured woman's point of view, but that's more difficult. I don't think you'd comprehend the motives of the white characters at all. You know it won't be so easy to explain the white girl's attitude, that is, so that her actions will seem credible to readers.

I didn't say it would be easy, he growled, but you don't need to exaggerate the difficulty.

Dear Byron, I'm just talking it over with you. I want to help you. What *is* her attitude?

Why, she loves the man!

Of course, but you've got to make readers *believe* that, believe, moreover that she's willing to brave race-prejudice and conventions that have risen from it. There's her family, for instance. . . .

God! he shouted. I don't get anything but discouragement out of you! At the same time he made a mental note that he must put the girl's father in the story.

Byron, she pleaded, please don't quarrel with me again. I can't bear it.

He was drawing on his overcoat and she grasped the sleeve in a pitiful gesture of appeal.

It seems, she went on sadly, that all we do lately is quarrel.

So it seems. He set his face hard.

Byron, I love you so much. I only want to help you. Won't you let me?

I don't want any of your help.

Byron!

You're ashamed of me because I'm not getting on as well as Howard!

Byron, *please!*

And you think Rudolph Fisher's a great writer because he's published a rotten story or two in the Atlantic!

She was silent.

I'll be damned if I'm going to stand your nagging any longer. I guess I know what I can do better than you do. You'll see! Wait till you read my story in a magazine! Then you'll be sorry.

Sorry! Dearest, I'll be delighted.

Sure you will . . . *not!* Let me go.

Byron, for once, be reasonable.

Let me go!

He tore away from her grasp and out of the door which he slammed behind him, but this time he felt a trifle ashamed of himself and lingered, hesitant, in the hallway, hoping, perhaps, that she would call him back. No sound, however, came from within. Tiptoeing to the door, he applied his ear to the keyhole. She was not crying; he could hear nothing. She really didn't love him at all. She just wanted to possess him, to own him, to boss him. He strode away in a renewed fit of fury and this time he did not turn back.

In his present mood he had no desire to return to his sordid hole in the wall. Finding a couple of dollars in his pocket, he determined to visit the Black Venus. He wanted to be cheered up and at this cabaret there was always excitement of some kind. Perhaps Irwin would be there, or Lucas Garfield. Perhaps a new golden-brown girl. He felt he wanted to be unfaithful to Mary, to degrade her ideal. He wanted to throw mud at everything she stood for. He'd like to tell her about it afterwards.

Preparing to descend the stairs that led to the cabaret, he was violently pushed aside. Two waiters were forcing a man out into the street. As they brushed past him Byron turned to see them deliver a final kick in the fellow's buttocks. Landing with a thud in the muddy gutter, the victim lay inert, apparently insensible. Byron felt sick. Life was so cruel. For the moment he experienced a pang of compassion for this stranger. I might be that man, he said to himself with a gush of self-pity.

In the dance hall his mood changed perceptibly. The room was crowded; all the tables were occupied with gay men and women, laughing, drinking. A yellow girl in red with a megaphone was making the rounds of the tables. As he stood, hesitating by the doorway, wondering if he could find a place, she shouted her song in his ear:

> She did me dirty,
> She did me wrong,
> She kept me fooled all along.
> But I've been so lonesome
> Since she went away
> That if she'll come home
> I'll let her stay . . .

I'll be three times God damned if I will! Byron gritted his teeth as he surrendered his coat to the girl in the check-room.

Dawggone, ef that ain't the cat's kanittans! a fat, cheerful-looking black man near him exclaimed.

Bardacious! agreed his companion.

Byron heard his name called: Dick was advancing towards him.

Hello, old chap!

Hello yourself! cried Byron, grasping his friend's hand. What in the world are you doing here?

Slumming. Brought some friends up with me. Come and sit with us. We've got plenty of gin.

I'd be glad to. I was wondering where I would sit. He hesitated before he inquired, Are you white or coloured tonight?

Buckra, of course. And so are my friends, but they'll be delighted to meet you. They've heard about the New Negro! Dick grinned.

Well, Byron replied, I don't feel very new tonight. I feel more like Old Black Joe. However, I'll do the best I can for your patronizing friends.

Dick was more sober at once. I didn't mean that, he assured Byron. They're not a bit that sort. They honestly, seriously want to meet some people, and I didn't know a soul in the place before you came.

Look at duh spagingy-spagade talkin' wid duh fagingy-fagade, Byron heard a voice behind him say.

Out fo' a little hootchie-pap, Ah *pre*-sume, another voice commented.

Well, evidently they don't see behind the mask even here, Byron said. He was in a better humour.

Of course not, Dick replied as he took his friend's

arm and led him to the table. His companions turned out to be Rusk Baldwin, the well-known columnist, and Roy McKain, the novelist. Byron recognized both names at once.

I can't see, McKain averred to Byron, after a few trivial remarks had passed back and forth, how fellows like you find anybody to talk to up here. Just look around! I'll bet you're the only college man in the place.

Oh, Byron knows a few, Dick remarked with a wink.

Well, it's wonderful up here, Baldwin exclaimed. I had no idea it would be like this. It's as wild as a jungle. Look at that waiter dancing the Charleston up the floor.

I don't see how he holds that tray of glasses, the novelist said. He doesn't spill a drop.

This remark reminded Dick that he had forgotten as yet to fill his friend's glass. He supplied his omission.

Can you Charleston, Mr. Kasson? Baldwin inquired.

Not very well, Byron responded.

McKain regarded him with unfeigned amazement. Why, he asserted, I thought all coloured people could dance the Charleston, didn't you, Dick?

I don't know much about it, was Dick's answer.

McKain poured out half a glass of gin and filled the receptacle to the brim with ginger ale. His enthusiasm mounted, soared.

I think you are a wonderful people, he announced, a perfectly wonderful people! Such verve and vivacity! Such dancing! Such singing! And I've always thought coloured people were lazy! I suppose, he added reflectively, that it's because you're all so happy. That's it, Rusk, he cried, they're all so happy!

Do you know the poems of a young coloured fellow named Langston Hughes? Baldwin demanded of Byron.

Yes, I do.

Well, I thought they were good before I came up here, but he's just a bus-boy or something like that, and he doesn't understand his race. Listen to this:

> My hands!
> My dark hands!
> Break through the wall!
> Find my dream!
> Help me to shatter this darkness,
> To smash this night,
> To break this shadow
> Into a thousand lights of sun,
> Into a thousand whirling dreams
> Of sun!

Well, I thought that was good, Baldwin repeated laughing, but now I see it's only bus-boy bunk. He don't understand his race.

I should say not, McKain agreed.

I took the trouble to learn it too, Baldwin continued. I thought it was good. Let's see, how does it go on?

> I lie down in the shadow.
> No longer the light of my dream before me,
> Above me.
> Only the thick wall.
> Only the shadow.

Bunk, echoed McKain. Bunk. It isn't a bit like that.

The entertainer had at last arrived at their table. Swaying back and forth, her eyes obliquely surveying the room, her mind apparently a vacuum, she howled through her megaphone:

> Did me dirty . . . did me wrong . . .

Pleasing sentiment, Baldwin remarked. How much shall I give her? he demanded of Byron.

Oh, half a dollar. A quarter. It doesn't matter.

McKain took out his purse and extracted a dollar bill.

Roy! some one across the room hailed him.

Why, there's Dana Paton, McKain cried. He's calling us over. He dragged Baldwin away with him.

They mean all right, Byron, Dick assured his friend apologetically.

I suppose they do, Byron replied, but I've had a

hell of a day and I guess I'm more nervous than usual. They're not bad . . . for ofays, he added.

His friend gave him a close scrutiny. You'd pass for Spanish or Portuguese, he assured him. Why don't you come over? There's no good bucking the game. It isn't worth it.

Byron's lip curled. I couldn't, he responded. I just couldn't. I don't blame you, or any one else who does, but I couldn't. I guess I haven't got the guts.

What you're doing requires more guts.

Don't let's talk about it, Byron urged impatiently.

As the music stopped, the laughter rose and fell. An atmosphere of fate hovered over the place, as if something were going to happen that nobody could prevent. Behind them a man sang softly to his companion:

> Firs' gal Ah love, she gi' me her right han',
> She's quit me in duh wrong for annuder man:
> Learn me to let all women alone.

Ha! Ha!

> Did you ever see yo' sweetie when her good man ain' aroun',
> Did you ever see yo' sweetie when her good man ain' aroun',
> Gits up in duh mawnin', turns duh feather bed upside down?

Now an amber searchlight shot across the room. The jazz band vomited, neighed, barked, and snorted and the barbaric ceremony began.

Dick pointed to a sinewy figure, fantastically garbed, making his way from the entrance across the floor. Look! he exclaimed. That's the Scarlet Creeper!

Who's he? Byron inquired.

Haven't you heard of the famous Creeper? Why he's the most celebrated character along Lenox Avenue. Lives off women, a true Eastman. He's the sheik of the dives, Anatole Longfellow by name.

As the Creeper eased past the dancers—so slinking and catlike was his gait that walking would scarcely describe it—they edged away from him, although there was a whispered recognition from nearly every couple in the hall. It was apparent that his entrance had caused a sensation and it was also quite evident that he was very contented with his reception. People might not speak to him, but they spoke about him. The Creeper was accompanied by a sinister, hunchback dwarf with a wizened, wrinkled, black face like a monkey's, the chin discoloured by a tetter, the head glowing with bushy, laniferous, silver hair. As the pair seated themselves at a recently deserted table adjoining that occupied by Byron and Dick three waiters immediately Charlestoned up.

This obviously explains the origin of the phrase "dancing attendance," Dick remarked.

The Creeper gave his orders in a consequential manner and the waiters hastened away to execute his commands. Byron and Dick were in a position where they might observe the fellow without seeming to do so. Apparently, he was making some faint effort to control his tone, but in order to make himself heard over the tipsy dignity of the jazz band, he was obliged to raise his voice which, moreover, was placed so excellently forward in his mouth that its resonance was double that of the ordinary organ.

Dat Nigger ain' got long ter live, the Creeper was announcing.

The hunchback cringed in mock dismay, as he rubbed his hands together and smiled his approval. Then, making a significant gesture with his right middle finger around his throat, he croaked, Ah bet you cut him every way but loose.

Carvin's too good fo' an achin' pain lak him. Ah'll git him wid a gun.

The hunchback rolled his eyes until only the whites were visible, the while he licked his thick, black lips with his fat, red tongue.

No man steal mah gal an' live, the Creeper went on. Dey'll soon be throwin' dirt in his face.

Dat Ruby's one God damn fool, the leering dwarf contributed. One God damn fool! he repeated, wagging his head savagely from side to side. He was almost in ecstasy.

The waiter returned with the drinks which he deposited on the table. The Creeper, having filled his own glass, contemptuously bestowed a few drops in that of his companion.

Well, whispered Byron, it looks bad for somebody.

Nothing but cheap boasting, Dick retorted. These shines that live off women are all cowards. He won't do a damn thing.

The Creeper had swirled into a dance with a handsome mulatto. His palms were flat across her shoulders, his slender fingers spread apart. There was an ancient impiety about the sensual grace of their united movement.

Take your eyes off the golden-brown, Dick warned, laughing.

You know my type!

It wouldn't take long to learn that.

Byron turned to his companion and looked at him earnestly. Dick, I want to ask you something, he said. Now . . . now . . . that you've gone white, do you really want . . . pinks for boody?

Dick averted his eyes. That's the worst of it, he groaned. I just don't. Give me blues every time.

Baldwin and McKain rejoined them.

Talking to a fellow who's making drawings, the novelist explained. God, but this place is great! I could live up here. Is all Harlem like this?

The question awakened a swarm of perverse, dancing images in Byron's brain. They crowded about each other, all the incongruities, the savage inconsistencies, the peculiar discrepancies, of this cruel, segregated life.

Yes, he replied, I suppose it is.

Four

Thoroughly ashamed of himself the next morning, Byron telephoned Mary, but the conversation was necessarily so unsatisfactory that in a measure he reverted to his recalcitrant mood. He knew full well, of course, that she could not speak freely over the telephone at the library, but even while his reason excused her, he was incapable of making the proper emotional adjustment. I'll show her, he assured himself. I'll show her. So he bowed his head over the blank sheet of paper lying before him on the table for the first time with a really vital interest in the undertaking.

He worked hard, in fact, all day, with a short respite for lunch—batter-bread and chittlings, which Mrs. Fox prepared for him—and by night had managed to turn out five or six pages of copy which he read over to himself not without satisfaction. He went out for dinner, but returned at an early hour to continue his labour throughout the evening. He passed another day in the same energetic manner. He found he could work like a demon once his interest and attention were won. By the close of the second day he had completed what he considered an extremely adequate version of the tale he had set himself to write.

He called on Mary that evening to tell her what he had done and for the first time in weeks they didn't quarrel.

I am so happy, dear, she said, and there were tears in her eyes.

Let me read it to you.

I'd love to have you.

After he had concluded the reading, she said, I am so proud of you, Byron. What are you going to do with it now?

He kissed her and explained, I'm going to take it to the Age office. I know a fellow over there who owns a machine he will let me use. After it's typed I'm going to send it to one of the big magazines.

I wish you all the luck in the world.

In a fever to get the manuscript off, he kissed her good-bye, and rushed away to the newspaper office. Later that night he mailed his typewritten story to a prominent magazine, enclosing, as he had been advised to do, a stamped and self-addressed envelope providing for its return in the unthinkable event of its refusal.

In two days it came back accompanied by a printed slip: Rejection of material does not imply lack of merit, etc. He carried this dejectedly to Mary, all his confidence gone.

Don't be discouraged, Byron dear, she urged him. Send it somewhere else. You may have to send it to a dozen magazines before it is accepted. See what the slip says. Doubtless the rejection is due to the fact that the editor has more copy piled up than he can use.

He followed her advice; apparently, there was no alternative procedure. Two days later, on his way out, he found the fat, white envelope in the box, and in the envelope another printed formula of rejection. This incident was repeated several times.

Meanwhile his funds were running low and it was paramount for him to discover some means of augmenting his income. He was too proud to appeal to the Sumners or any other of his father's successful friends. He could not bear to let them know that he needed any assistance.

One night while the girls were dressing preparatory to going out, he found himself alone with Howard in the little sitting-room.

Old fellow, Howard began, diffidently enough, you know I'm going to make a barrel of money now that I'm Pettijohn's attorney. I've already received a considerable advance. Won't you let me lend you a hundred?

Howard too! Everybody patronized him.

I don't need your money, he replied stiffly. I can get along all right by myself.

Howard was not to be so easily repulsed. See here, old boy, he insisted, you can't talk to me like that. If I needed it and you had it, I'd come to you. What have you got your back up for?

Byron's back was no longer up. He broke down

and cried, his arms sprawled across the table.

He accepted the money.

Again began the weary round. Every day he went through the agony of visiting the employment agencies, searching, searching. Some firms refused to employ a Negro. When they were tolerant in this respect it often happened that he was ignorant of the technique of the business. Occasionally a prospective employer found him too well dressed, too well educated. We just want Southern darkies who are willing to work, was the tactful explanation. It was no good to give these individuals assurance of his readiness to comply. Sometimes they considered him too dark in colour; at other times, too light.

Once Mary tried to help. Discovering that a certain professor engaged in research work needed a secretary, she urged him to send for Byron, but the professor had not been warned and when he greeted Byron with, So you're the young man Mary Love has recommended, Byron stormed out of the office and refused to return. As a result of this incident he had another furious scene with Mary. Thereafter, she made no further attempt to aid him.

During this period there were recurrent nights of dissipation, cabarets, sessions in pool-rooms and at the Commonwealth Club, drink, and occasionally, casual golden-browns.

At last one morning, making his invariable search in the mail-box, he found a letter. The envelope was stamped with the name of the latest magazine to which he had dispatched his story. As he tore the flap open, his fingers trembled. He read the contents over at least twenty times.

My dear Mr. Kasson, they ran:

Will you please call to see me at your earliest convenience in regard to the story you sent me.

very truly,

RUSSETT DURWOOD

editor.

Little Byron play on your harp! he cried aloud, and then tore down the street towards the library. He found Mary at her desk.

Mary! Mary! he cried, thrusting the letter in her face.

She read it at a glance.

Byron, she exclaimed, this is simply wonderful!

You didn't read it, he complained.

Why, of course, I did.

Well, read it again.

She obeyed him, to please him, scanning it more carefully this time, as if it were couched in obscure terms.

I'm so proud of you, she assured him.

You said I couldn't do it. You didn't believe in me. I told you I'd show you.

I *hoped* you could do it, Byron. You can't realize how delighted I am that you have succeeded. When are you going to see him?

Now! He says at my earliest convenience. At once! This minute! Good-bye! I'll call you up later. He rushed out of the library.

A half-hour later he walked into the office of the American Mars and asked the boy at the desk if he might see the editor. The boy responded by pushing a blank form across the desk with the nonchalant instruction, Fill that out. Byron obeyed. The boy disappeared with the slip of paper, to return presently with the invitation, Follow me.

Byron had not expected to meet so young a man. Russett Durwood possessed the sort of round, kind face to which widows might confide their secrets. His eyes were the colour that painters employ to suggest spring skies. His light-brown hair was parted in the middle smoothly over his heavy brow. His ears were prominent features. Between the fingers of his right hand he held a large, unlighted, black cigar which he flourished as he talked, or else sucked meditatively. His feet were planted on his scrupulously clean desk.

Shaking hands with Byron, he invited him to sit down.

I asked you to come in about your story, Durwood began in his resonant and cheerful voice.

Yes, Byron replied, with such eagerness that the tone trembled.

Durwood turned away and gazed out of the window. The view, terraces piled on terraces, was certainly worthy of his attention. Presently, he looked back at the figure before him.

I am very much interested in Negro literature; that's why I sent for you, the editor continued. He appeared to be in no manner of hurry, but Byron made no reply. . . . Also, Durwood went on, after a pause, when I see a fellow with talent going the wrong way, I try to be honest. It pays better in the end. It's more useful to you, too, he said, at once giving his remarks a more personal slant. Byron felt his heart thumping. . . . What I want to know is this: why in hell don't you write about something you know about? Without waiting for a response, he continued rapidly, I happen to be acquainted to some extent with Negro life. I am proud to call certain Negroes my friends. I have visited Harlem in two capacities, as a customer in the cabarets and as a guest in my friends' homes. The whole place, contrary to the general impression, is overrun with fresh, unused material. Nobody has yet written a good gambling story; nobody has touched the outskirts of cabaret life; nobody has gone into the curious subject of the divers tribes of the region. Why, there are West Indians and Abyssinian Jews, religious Negroes, pagan Negroes, and Negro intellectuals, all living together more or less amicably in the same community, each group with its own opinions and atmosphere and manner of living; each individual with his own opinions and atmosphere and manner of living. But

I find that Negroes don't write about these matters; they continue to employ all the old clichés and formulas that have been worried to death by Nordic blonds who, after all, never did know anything about the subject from the inside. Well, if you young Negro intellectuals don't get busy, a new crop of Nordics is going to spring up who will take the trouble to become better informed and will exploit this material before the Negro gets around to it. Do you know why I sent you a letter instead of merely returning your manuscript with a rejection slip? he inquired suddenly.

Byron shook his head.

It's because I believe you can write. Why, the passage describing the white lad's emotions when he learns about his sister's engagement is positively Conradian. It's marvellously done, not a word too much or too little. Full of suggestion and psychologically true. You must have spent a lot of time with white people to understand them so well.

Byron looked blank.

Too much time, Durwood added, chewing savagely at the end of his cigar. The coloured parts, on the other hand, are terrible. Why don't you learn something about your people? A Methodist cab-driver would hoot at your prostitute. She's as solemn as a column-conductor. Your Negro intellectual is a little better, but I must say that although my personal acquaintance with Negro intellectuals is somewhat broad, I've never met one before who was made entirely out of wood. This hero of yours is as pious as the pope, so damned good that he becomes absolutely idiotic. He speaks in platitudes and when he walks the hinges in his legs creak. Now just look at this page. . . . Durwood opened the manuscript . . . Did you ever read the Rollo books?

No sir.

Well, you don't need to. You've written one yourself on this page. God, boy, let your characters live and breathe! Give 'em air. Let 'em react to life and talk and act naturally. You've got an idea here, but it's a dangerous idea. Damned hard not to make it melodrama or cheap propaganda. Hardly an experienced writer in the whole world would dare tackle it. I can't think of any one who could make a go of it. Let me see . . . He appeared to be reflecting . . . No, I can't think of any one. Well, that's what I mean. Select a subject you're full of, inside and out, and then consider carefully whether it's a subject safe for an inexperienced writer to handle. You must have a hundred better ideas in your head. Are you a college man?

Yes, I am.

I thought so. Writers should never go to college. It does 'em up for two years after they get out. They think in terms of the professors and remember all the rotten rules. Bunk! Pishposh!

But you must have some life of your own. Do you live in Harlem?

Yes.

I wouldn't have believed it! Ever been to a cabaret?

Many times.

Well, that I *can't* believe! Jean Cocteau could have done a cabaret better without ever having heard of such a dive. Your scene reads like a description of a Baptist sociable for the new minister. You'll have to learn to be more observing. This story obviously is not autobiographical. Why don't you write about some experience of your own?

I don't think anything very interesting ever happens to me.

All the better! Nothing like a dull life as the inspiration for fine fiction. Huysmans constructed a whole novel around the birth of a calf and the death of a cat. But, good God, man, if you object to dulness in literature, look around you. Harlem life isn't dull. It has more aspects than a diamond has facets. Do you know anything about Marcus Garvey?

Not very much, I'm afraid.

That's a pity . . . Durwood sighed . . . I'd like to find a good character study of *him*. Well, it doesn't matter. There's plenty of other copy. There's the servant-girl, for instance. Nobody has ever done the Negro servant-girl, who refuses to "live in." Washing dishes in the day-time, she returns at night to her home in Harlem where she smacks her daddy in the jaw or else dances and makes love. On the whole I should say she has the best time of any domestic servant in the world. Know anything about the fast set?

Not very much.

Too bad you don't know more. The Negro fast set does everything the Long Island fast set does, plays bridge, keeps the bootlegger busy, drives around in Rolls-Royces, and commits adultery, but it is vastly more amusing than the Long Island set for the simple reason that it is *amused*.

After all, the main thing is to use your eyes and your brain. Why, Roy McKain visited Harlem just once and then brought me in a capital yarn about a Negro pimp. I don't suppose he even saw the fellow. Probably just made him up, imagined him, but his imagination was based on a background of observation. The milieu is correct. The story is credible. It jumps ahead; it lives. I'm featuring it in the June number.

Durwood yawned. Well, I don't suppose I've got anything more to say to you. I don't want to flatter you, because I honestly believe you ought to have your throat cut for turning in such an atrocity as this story, but it's an actual fact that I haven't wasted so much time giving an author advice in the last three years. I usually take 'em or leave 'em. There's no good arguing with authors. A sour and disorderly bunch. However, when I read that passage in your tale, I said to myself, That boy's got something if he can see the light.

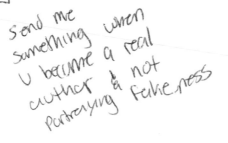

Go home now, tear up everything you've written, and begin afresh. Pray and get drunk. Send me something else some time when you've decided to become a regular author and not a pseudo-literary fake. Good morning.

Five

How he got out of that office, out of that building, Byron never knew. He was only conscious that he was striding rapidly up Sixth Avenue. His head was whirling with a confusion of emotions; disappointment dominated them, cruel heartbreaking disappointment. He began to feel sorry for himself. Self-pity surged into his heart. Why should he, who had talent and energy, he who had tried to do something worth while, be made to suffer, to eat mud? He treated me that way because I am a Negro! was his subsequent passionate conclusion. He wouldn't dare talk like that to a white man. His fury was a flame that scorched him.

Suddenly he stood still. Should he go back? Should he tell Durwood what he thought of him? What good? He realized his impotence. They wouldn't let him in the office. He was a Negro and he was alone. Groaning, he burned to summon up a mob to stamp out this proud, haughty white world. He yearned to tear New York apart stone by stone, to level the houses one by one, to trample these white fiends under foot.

Stumping along the sidewalk, an old Negro with

a long white beard approached with the aid of a cane. Uncle Tom! Old Black Joe! One of those damn conciliatory Niggers who "knew their places," who conformed.

He became aware that his hand still grasped the envelope containing his story. Should he destroy it? What was the use of his writing? No chance. No opportunity. Nothing but work on an elevator for such as he!

When he thought of Mary, fiery demons danced before his eyes: she had been the first to try to discourage him. She had told him first what this swine in a swivel-chair had just thrown in his face. He had promised to telephone her. He'd be damned if he would keep that promise. He'd be glad to rot in hell if he ever wanted to see her silly Madonna face again, always so superior. She sneered, that's what she did, she sneered. He was through.

He strode on, automatically, knowing neither where nor why. Faster and faster he paced up the Avenue. What could he do next? He was no manual labourer. He had proved himself a failure at that. Why, no one would even give him a job. Too damn swell to be a longshoreman and not swell enough for any position for which his education fitted him. [Wrong colour.]

Just another Nigger, and so they push, and buffet, and kick me about. Go live somewhere else and do something else! Where? What? Mary wanted him to know the Sumners. God damn snobs, that's what they were! God damn snobs! He hated them all, black and white alike. All conspiring to effect his downfall. All ready to give him one more hard knock. No help, no hope, anywhere. Just another Nigger!

At Fifty-ninth Street an altercation between two street-vendors arrested his attention. Their carts were drawn up one behind the other close to the kerb, and the great white horse attached to the inferior cart was placidly munching the bright crimson heads of the potted geraniums on the forward cart. The florist, an Italian, was screaming with rage, hurling unintelligible epithets at the little Jew who owned the white horse. The Jew laughed and made no effort to back his cart. Suddenly the Italian drew a long knife from his belt and plunged it to the hilt into the breast of the animal. The beast groaned sickishly and shuddered, but did not fall. The blood gushed out in a great red stream, like water from a hydrant. Blood! Blood! It flooded the pavement. The sheeny was screaming. A crowd collected. They were pounding the dago.

Byron stumbled on. The day, though bright with sunshine, was cold, the air brisk and stiffening, but Byron was so hot that he removed his overcoat. Blood! He thought he was going to vomit. Blood and cruelty.

He was in an impasse. He could think of no

solution save to go back home and confess himself a failure and that in itself would be no solution. That meant that he had to begin all over again somewhere else in this heartless world of blacks, near whites, and whites. This world where they stabbed horses who were eating geraniums. Flinging himself on a Park bench, he buried his face in his hands.

He was awakened by a cry which his subconsciousness warned him was addressed to him. He looked up to stare at a halted automobile. In the open doorway eyes flashed under a sable toque and a gloved hand beckoned. He did not recognize what he could see of the face: the great collar of a sable coat protected the chin and caressed the cheek. Nevertheless, he responded to the summons.

You! he exclaimed.

Yes, Lasca replied. Jump in. I'm chilled to the bone and I want to close the door.

He obeyed her. The chauffeur drove on.

What on earth are you doing in the Park at this hour in the morning? she demanded. Have you become a forester or a landscape gardener?

I must have been waiting for you! His spirits were rising. As he sank back into the grateful luxury of the soft cushions next to this lovely animal swathed in sables, she tucked the robe of leopard-fur around his legs.

I've telephoned you several times, he announced.

I've been out of town, amusing myself until my apartment was ready. I can't stand too much of Sylvia; she gets on my nerves. Do you know her?

Not very well.

I'm about fed up with her. She whines. So I went to Atlantic City.

But your apartment?

Oh, that was all arranged while I was away. I merely told a decorator what I wanted, et voila! She made such a gesture with her hand as, on the stage, Jane Cowl would have made after such a phrase. He had seen the actress do this. With the grand manner in real life he was more unfamiliar.

Directly I've done an errand, she went on, I'm going back there. Will you come with me?

Ask me!

Byron felt soothed, smoothed the right way, for the first time in weeks. Luxury, as a matter of fact always soothed him when he did not resent its implications. Somehow with Lasca he resented nothing. She was rich, amusing, soft to the touch, beautiful, sympathetic, fragrant with what he supposed to be the latest perfume from Paris.

When the motor stopped before a smart dressmaker's on Fifty-seventh Street, Lasca got out of the car and entered the shop. She returned in exactly ten minutes.

They've just received some new importations from Paris. I've found two gowns that will do.

But don't you have to try them on?

Oh, I'll do that at home. I can't be bothered taking my clothes off here. Nobody in that shop sufficiently interests me. Just a bunch of sissies!

You're wonderful! was all that it occurred to Byron to say.

She regarded him quizzically. Seems to me I've heard that before, somewhere, she remarked, and then, You're more cheerful now.

How did you know . . . ? he demanded in astonishment.

I ordered the car stopped a full thirty seconds before I called to you, and even so I had to call twice. You appeared to be extremely despondent, almost as if you had made up your mind to throw yourself into the lake.

I *was* despondent. I never thought of suicide before, but . . .

What's the trouble?

I've had a rotten deal all around. It's hell to be a Negro in this world.

She stared at him fixedly as if she were about to reply to this statement, but apparently she changed her mind. Presently she said, You dance well. I particularly remember your dancing.

So do you. I've thought of nothing else since. I've called you up . . .

So you told me. Let's dance together again. Ever go to the Winter Palace?

No. Can't afford it.

Never been to the Winter Palace! But, boy, you must come, you must come as my guest.

I'd love to.

Through her cloak, under the leopard-skin robe, he was conscious of her nearness. The physical vitality of the woman was electric.

What's become of that funny girl you were with the night I met you—Mary what's her name?

She's all right, I guess. I don't see her.

Snooty, little prig, I thought. Ugh! I detest the type. They've done nothing—always been protected and sheltered—and they're so damn superior.

This statement of the case exactly coincided with Byron's present opinion, but curiously he was annoyed to hear it from Lasca's lips.

She's all right, I guess. I don't see her, he repeated dully.

Let's forget about her, Lasca said, as she drew his hand into hers. She was staring squarely into his eyes and he observed, to his amazement, that her own lustrous eyes were wet with tears.

God, but you're wonderful! he cried, returning the pressure of her fingers.

She immediately withdrew her hand, at the same time shifting the position of her leg.

Atlantic City is lovely, she remarked in a cold, distant tone. I have so many friends there.

Do you like it as well as New York?

Oh, I don't care where I am, or, very often, with whom. I find what I want everywhere.

You're rich, Byron remarked, with a tinge of bitterness. It's easy for you.

I haven't always been rich, Byron, but I've always found what I wanted—even money.

You're luckier than most—than most Negroes anyway.

Negroes aren't any worse off than anybody else. They're better off, if anything. They have the same privileges that white women had before the bloody fools got the ballot. They're considered irresponsible like children and treated with a special fondness. Why, in Harlem one is allowed to do thousands of things that one would get arrested for downtown. Take the game of Numbers; everybody plays Numbers, and yet it is just a lottery and consequently against the law. . . . Of course, she continued, after a slight pause, I've never bothered very much about the fact that I'm coloured. It doesn't make any difference to me and I've never thought very much about it. I do just what I want to.

But how can you? What about discrimination? Segregation?

They just don't exist for me. I wouldn't tolerate such a thing. I live in New York exactly as I live in Paris. I do just what I want to and go where I please—to any theatre or hotel—and get what I'm after. You see, most Negroes are so touchy and nervous that they obey the unwritten Jim Crow laws—you must remember that any form of discrimination is quite illegal in New York—to escape getting hurt. Nobody *can* hurt me, and so, of course, nothing unpleasant ever happens to me.

Don't you ever get bored?

Unmercifully. Sometimes, I think I'd like to die, I get so bored. It's so tiresome to be uniformly successful. I get so fed up with life that I could scream, but something—well, something always happens to bring me back, a new thrill, a new dress, a new dog—something. I've never been bored long and I never will be. . . . She tapped on wood with her gloved hand. . . . I won't permit myself to be bored, she announced, almost sternly. It's a weakness, my only one, she muttered under her breath.

You're a wonderful woman! Byron apparently could muster up no alternative approbatory phrase.

So you've said, and you're quite right. I don't know any other who is quite so wonderful. Fortunately, she continued, there are wonderful men too.

She gave vent to a hearty laugh. Her mirth proved infectious. Without much knowing why, without much caring why, Byron yielded to her mood. This time, it was he who sought her hand.

He had never before seen a chamber so magnificent as Lasca's drawing-room. The walls, tinted an apple-green, were bare of pictures, save the representation of a nude woman in a silver frame which hung over the white marble fireplace. The French furniture was upholstered in rich brocades of lemon and old rose. Over the Steinway, a black Spanish shawl, embroidered in huge vermilion and orange flowers, was held in place by a rock-crystal lamp in the form of a Chinese goddess. Strewn on the tables, the desk, the mantelpiece, were more Chinese objects, birds, fish and animals, scent-bottles, carved out of ivory, jade, malachite, and moss-agate. On one of the tables stood a blue porcelain bowl filled with yellow roses, roses with so few petals that they resembled wild flowers. They had a strangely naïve air in this artificial environment. Transparent curtains of lemon yellow hung at the windows and sprawled on the jade-green carpet like the trains of ladies' dresses in 1896, and behind them, towards the light, depended further curtains of rose and deep-blue. Although the sun was shining brightly outside, only a soft light filtered through them into the room.

Byron completed his admiring appraisal by lifting the cover of a heavy, Russian cigarette box of silver, and extracting a cigarette. As he lighted a match, Lasca returned. The cigarette dropped from his nervous fingers. He stooped to recapture it.

That's right! Don't burn my carpet, she urged.

You're so beautiful!

She was wearing a dressing-gown of soft, filmy golden-brown chiffon, adorned with bands of ostrich-feather filaments which graduated in colour from a pale yellow near her throat to a fiery orange about her ankles. Her golden-brown arms were bare; her feet were shod in golden mules.

She was followed almost immediately by the maid, bearing a tray containing glasses and a silver bucket of ice in which two bottles were chilling.

Bring the table over here, Lasca commanded, sinking back into a divan banked with lemon and rose cushions.

Sit down, she invited Byron as she lighted a cigarette.

He obeyed her while the maid, lifting one of the bottles, tenderly wrapped a napkin around its belly, and coaxed the cork out. It emerged with a lusty pop to strike the crystal chandelier, causing a great jangling among the pendents.

Brava, Marie! Lasca laughed.

When the maid had departed, Lasca proposed a toast: To crime and punishment!

Crime and punishment?

Yes. Our crime and the punishment of the innocent. They should always be punished. It's so easy *not* to do anything. But the guilty! . . . Her eyes sparkled. . . . I'm for them!

They drank the toast.

You haven't kissed me yet, she remarked in a perfectly casual tone.

It seemed to Byron that his blood would burst from his arteries. Clasping her in his arms, holding her tightly pressed against his body, almost reclining now, he sought her lips.

After a little she pushed him gently away.

You kiss very well, she remarked.

Lasca! I adore you! I want you always!

I'm not going to leave you, she assured him, and now, for the first time he noted a strange, musical throbbing in her voice, and I'm not going to let you go. Didn't I tell you that I always get what I want.

But why do you want *me?* What can I give to *you?*

She poised his head between her palms and spoke in a voice raucous with passion: I want you to possess me, to own me. I want to be your slave, your Nigger, your own Nigger!

As Lasca drew her body a little apart from Byron, she inquired, Aren't you hungry?

I don't know. I'm much too happy to know. I love you!

He kissed her throat reverently; it was almost as if it were a ceremony.

So you'd better. You'll never find any one like me for love. I'll spoil all the others for you.

You have already. Oh, Lasca, I want you and nobody but you.

Well, you have me—now.

Promise me it will be for ever.

Yes, yes, of course it will, she replied impatiently, as she pressed the button on her bed-table. She did not shift her position when the maid entered. While she ordered lunch Byron's head lay cushioned on her shoulder.

They reclined under a spread of grey and silver and rose Spanish brocade, with a deep flounce of silver Spanish lace. The room itself was delicate and fragile, all silver and grey silk and crystal pendents, with here and there a note of rose. The heavy curtains were drawn. The chamber was lighted by side lamps softened by rose shades.

Where do you live? Lasca demanded unexpectedly.

He told her.

I'll send Harry for your clothes.

alliteration of S

Six

A very black fellow, six feet tall, in a purple uniform ornamented with gold braid, guarded the door, but he bowed low as Lasca and Byron approached the entrance and waved them in. At the foot of the stairway, they were subjected to a second scrutiny through the bars of a window in the upper half of another door.

Mrs. Sartoris, come right in, the defender of the portal cried, and, as they accepted the invitation, he called out: Table for Mr. Gunnion!

A waiter took up the cry.

Come right this way, Mr. Gunnion, he urged, and led the pair to a table directly opposite the band.

Why Mr. Gunnion? Byron demanded of Lasca as they seated themselves.

She laughed and threw back her green velvet evening cloak embroidered in silver flowers.

That's part of the code here, she explained. If you're Mr. Gunnion it means that you're a good spender and a generally desirable customer, so you get the best available table. If you're Mr. Lomax, you're lucky if you even get in.

But they don't even know me! he protested.

You're with Mrs. Gunnion tonight.

Seated at tables around the three sides of the hall unoccupied by the band, were parties of white people, parties of coloured people, mixed parties, but the amber light which flooded the gold and black hall gave everybody present much the same complexion, save one brown girl who had put on too much powder and consequently looked dirty green.

In the centre of the dance floor, a sinewy, male dancer, hair sleek and oiled, was performing the Charleston.

> Hey! Hey!
> I'm Charleston crazy!

Buddy, I'm with you! cried Lasca, as she stepped on to the floor.

The crowd applauded her appearance. Some one cried, Strut your stuff, Lasca!

> Hey! Hey!
> I'm going to Charleston back to Charleston!

Lasca tossed her heels back and danced with the utmost abandon.

> Hey! Hey!
> Do that thing!

Camel walk!

Pull 'em down!

Pick cherries!

She lifted her short skirt of champagne-coloured

crêpe high over her knees. A ruby set in platinum flashed its fire below her elbow. Her head was encased in a cloche of emerald-green.

As she returned to her table amidst a flurry of applause and laughter, the waiter bore in a bucket of ice from which a bottle-neck protruded. The manager of the Winter Palace, a dapper fellow, joined them.

Well, he exclaimed, I'm delighted. How's the little lady tonight?

How are you, Danny? She shook his hand. Sit down and meet Mr. Kasson.

My compliments. He lounged into the seat beside her. Delighted to see the little lady again. When you come in the lights are brighter and the band really works.

Behave, Danny. Say, has Sid been here? Her brow was clouded by a frown.

Not yet.

Don't let him in, see!

I get you.

Well, fill up! Lasca poured out the glasses. Then, raising her own, she proposed, Tea for three!

Byron emptied his glass at one swallow.

Got any happy dust, Danny? Lasca inquired.

Anything the little lady wants.

Send Myra to the lady's room.

Lasca preceded the vendor. Danny whistled until he attracted the attention of the cigarette-girl who nodded in reply to his signal.

First time here, Mr. Kasson?

Yes.

Well, you must come often.

Say, it's great. Is it always like this?

Wait awhile. You ain't seen nothing yet.

Byron looked around the room. He observed Piqua St. Paris and Arabia Scribner sitting with two men whom he did not recognize. Monte Esbon and a party occupied another table.

Presently Lasca returned.

Who's that punkin-seed sheik in the corner? she demanded.

Nothing for the little lady, Danny responded. He's queer.

Lasca grinned. Is Ran here yet? she asked.

No, Danny replied. He never gets here much before two.

I want to see him.

He'll want to see you.

Why, there's Monte! she cried, waving her hand.

Monte came over. Hello, Lasca! Hello, Byron! Some hoofer, Lasca! How you can shake your dogs!

Bottle it, Monte. How do you like my dress?

Nothing else but.

So's your old man.

Be your age! If you knew what I was thinkin' you'd lock me up.

Danny, having imbibed three-quarters of the contents of the bottle of champagne, begged to be excused. I've got to look out for some of my other guests, he explained. I'll be back.

Danny's a wonder, Lasca commented. He runs from table to table lapping up the expensive drinks. The customers hardly get a look-in on their own liquor. Another quart of Lanson 1914, she commanded the waiter, and ask Toscanini to play my favourite tune.

As the waiter whispered in his ear, the pianist gave his men their cue and the band broke into, I like pie, I like cake.

It's a grand symphony! cried Lasca. Ta! Ta! Monte. Come back later.

She led Byron to the floor.

Black Bottom, she whispered.

I can't do it very well, he protested.

Try it, she adjured him.

Strangely enough, he found it perfectly simple to execute the intricate steps under the inspiring influence of her example. The floor was not crowded; only three or four couples were dancing. The music was soft and sensual; the band knew all the tricks of jazz, but it was a jazz made exquisite, refined. The saxophone cooed like a turtle dove, the drumbeat seemed to reverberate from a distance.

As Byron's lips brushed Lasca's cheek, an exotic fragrance assailed his nostrils, a fragrance with which he was becoming more and more familiar, a fragrance it would be impossible henceforth for him to forget.

Coty? he whispered interrogatively.

No, body, she lisped.

Now they were dancing more slowly, lifting one leg while they swayed to the opposite side. They were as close together as two individuals can ever be. He was fascinated by her sense of rhythm, captivated by her personality, intoxicated by her magnetism.

As they swayed around the hall, his eyes caught those of Piqua St. Paris. She was looking straight at him, but she gave no sign of recognition. He shifted his gaze to Mrs. Scribner. She stared at him fixedly for a moment, and then turned ostentatiously away. Indubitably they had, both of them, cut him dead. What did it mean? What had he done? He could think of no reason to ascribe to their action. Well, what did it matter? Mind soul, and body, he belonged to Lasca. No use trying to think; no use trying to do anything but drift, drift, on this barge of pleasure bound for Cythera. The wind was favourable, the signs and tokens propitious.

As they returned to their table a stout entertainer in bright orange, began to shout:

> You ain't gonna ride no chariot tonight
> 'Less you take your sweet mama along!
> I say, Ben Hur, you ain't goin' out
> Till you listen to this song.
> I know you been drivin'
> To some other girl's door,

But I'm gonna see to it
You don't drive there no more.
You ain't gonna ride no chariot tonight
'Less you take your sweet mama along.

Here's Ran, Danny came up to announce. Looking towards the entrance Byron saw the Bolito King, imposing with his gold cane and silk hat. He was accompanied by a girl. Waving his hand at Lasca, he escorted his companion to a table in the far end of the room, and then walked towards them.

How you been, Mrs. Sartoris? he demanded, nodding casually at the same time in Byron's general direction.

Fine, Rannie. Sit down. Who's the skirt?

Oh, dat's jes' little Ruby. Nobody you know.

Better be-have, Ran.

Oh, Ah's one o' duh best be-havers 'roun' dis place.

A shriek interrupted them. Instinctively they turned to see what was happening. A yellow girl at a table nearby had risen and stood facing another woman seated with two men.

Ah'll turn yo' damper down! she screamed.

Ah'll cut you every way but loose! the other retorted.

Lemme miss you.

Run 'roun' duh block an' git yo'self some air.

At this precise juncture, the man sitting on the outside of the table jumped up and hurled a glass full of whiskey with unsteady aim. It shivered against the mirror while the ineffectual assailant crumbled on the floor exactly as though he had been hit. Two waiters caught him under the arm-pits and dragged him outside. The yellow girl followed him, screaming. The woman left behind called out to the retreating male figure, Lemme see duh back o' yo' white collar an' den Ah knows you's goin'.

During this scene, the Bolito King sat smoking unconcernedly, quite as if he were unaware that anything unusual had occurred.

Hey! Hey! Do that thing!

Well, I guess Ah'll ramble back to Ruby, Mr. Pettijohn announced. How long you stayin', Mrs. Sartoris?

Till the dawn comes up like thunder.

Another entertainer had the floor.

Born an' bred in Harlem,
Harlem to duh bone,
Ah say, born an' bred in Harlem,
Harlem to duh bone,
Early every mornin'
You can hear me moan:

Ah'm a hard-boiled mama
From Lenox Avenue.
'Tain't nobody's business
What Ah do.
Sometimes Ah feels lonesome,
Sometimes Ah feels sad,
But Ah can't keep no lover
Cause Ah's evil an' bad.

Ah found me a papa,
A high yaller too.
He lef' me in duh mornin'
With his face all black an' blue
Ah drinks bad liquor
An' Ah likes et strong.
Ah'm a hard-boiled mama,
So doan do me no wrong.

Shake 'em out! went the cry. Strut your stuff! The little dancer was lean and yellow, dressed in scarlet; her pink drawers were adorned with blue forget-me-nots. Her legs were like toothpicks.

Oh, gaze on dat wobble, man!

Too skinny, Danny, Lasca complained to the manager who was passing the table.

Wait! he adjured her.

Presently the dancer went into a shivering ecstasy. From the top of her head to her feet she quivered. It was like an enjoyable ague.

Lasca tossed a crumpled dollar bill on the floor. Stamping her heel squarely over the vail, the girl continued her strange, seismic performance as she shouted:

Ah can shake et up,
Ah can shake et down,
Ah can put et on duh flo'
An' turn et roun'.

I'm sick of entertainers, Danny, Lasca cried. Put on your old band.

Danny gave the signal and the crowd surged over the floor. The dancing was becoming wilder. There were camel-walkers, symptoms of the twa-twa and the skate. A pretty mulatto broke away from her partner and moved her hands convulsively up and down her body in the throes of the itch.

Hug me warmer, baby, Lasca begged.

Love me? Byron queried.

Red hot with love!

What are they playing?

She sang the words:

> I looked at the clock and the clock struck three;
> I said, now daddy, that's one on me.

The clock struck four, protested Byron.

That's all right. It'll strike ten before we're through.

I'll never say Amen!

Don't boast. I've worn out better men than you.

Later, Byron's vision became somewhat blurred and his hearing inaccurate. He had a confused sense that all the instruments and human voices in the place were shrieking simultaneously. There was a constant beating of the drum. No longer were the dancers in pairs; apparently they had become quartets. Curious and unaccountable streaks of light wrinkled the faces of the mirrors. People appeared to be shuffling at peculiarly acute angles. Would they topple over?

Lasca poured out champagne from the fifth bottle.

Le's drink a little before we go on! Le's have a drink.

She was lying in Byron's arms, frequently seeking his mouth.

Break away! Time! Byron heard Monte, passing the table, admonish them.

Music! I jesh love music, was all Byron could think of to say.

It was six o'clock when, with some assistance from one of the waiters, he emerged from the Winter Palace. He thanked the cold morning air for blowing in his face.

Taxi! Lasca was crying, apparently as fresh as when she had started out.

Have a whiff of snow, she urged him as they sat in the taxicab, his head nestled in her bosom.

Gimme, he muttered feebly.

From a packet she sifted a line of white crystals along her first finger.

Sniff the happy dust, baby. It'll make you feel better.

He made the effort. A cool, refreshing sniff—like water from a spring.

Opening the door of the cab, the chauffeur stuck his head through the aperture.

Would you parties mind tellin' me where you wants to go? he demanded.

> I looked at the clock and the clock struck six;
> I said, Now daddy, do you know any more tricks?
> While he was . . .

Quite unexpectedly, Byron revived. He was restored, energetic.

Drive to hell! he cried.

Yes, drive to hell! Lasca echoed.

To hell! To hell! On to hell!

To hell with red hot mama and cold weather papa!

I'm not cold weather papa! he protested.

The chauffeur scratched his head. I guess you means duh Black Mass.

He started the car.

What's that? Byron inquired.

It's a garden where champagne flows from all the fountains and the paths are made of happy dust and the perfume of the poppies is opium. Kiss me!

I'd like to be cruel to you! she cried, after she had momentarily slaked her thirst. I'd like to cut your heart out!

Cut it out, Lasca, my own! It belongs to you!

I'd like to bruise you!

Lasca, adorable!

I'd like to gash you with a knife!

Lasca! Lasca!

Beat you with a whip!

Lasca!

She drew her pointed nails across the back of his hand. The flesh came off in ribbons.

My baby! My baby! she sobbed, binding his bleeding hand with her handkerchief, kissing his lips.

Emerging from the cab, her dress caught in the door frame, and was torn straight down the front. She ripped off a yard or so of dangling crêpe.

I'll go naked to the Black Mass! she cried, as she extracted a dollar bill from her gold bag and handed it to the chauffeur.

They stood before a heavy unlighted portal. Lasca sought the push-button and pressed it rapidly eight times. Presently the door swung open and they faced utter darkness. She pulled Byron in after her and slammed the door behind them, an action, apparently, which automatically lighted the hallway. They walked down this long corridor, like a tunnel. At the further end was another door, protected by a heavy velvet curtain which Lasca brushed aside. She gave seven rapid knocks. A panel slid open; an eye appeared; this door too swung on its hinges.

They had not yet heard a sound, but now they were aware of music and laughter, uncanny, horrible laughter. A silent attendant, in red doublet and hose, deprived them of their wraps, and led them to still a third door which, when opened, disclosed a cabinet particulier painted a deep blue. It would seem they had been expected: wine and food appeared so immediately. The horrid laughter and the music persisted, drifting in from behind a curtain which walled one side of the room. Suddenly it stopped.

Come, said Lasca, after they had each drunk a glass of champagne, and she led him through a parting in this curtain.

They stood in a circular hall entirely hung in vermilion velvet; even the ceiling was draped in this fiery colour. The room, indeed, resembled a tent. The floor was of translucent glass, and through this clouds of light flowed, now orange, now deep purple, now flaming like molten lava, now rolling sea-waves of green. An invisible band, silent at the moment they had entered this deserted room, now began to perform wild music, music that moaned and lacerated one's breast with brazen claws of tone, shrieking, tortured music from the depths of hell. And now the hall became peopled, as dancers slipped through the folds of the hangings, men and women with weary faces, faces tired of passion and pleasure. Were these the faces of dead prostitutes and murderers? Pleasure seekers from the cold slabs of the morgue?

Dance! cried Lasca. Dance! She flung herself in his arms and they joined this witches' sabbath. Demoniac saxophones wailed like souls burning in an endless torment. Triumphant trumpets called to a profane glory. Byron offered himself freely to the conforming curves of her sensual body, delivered himself to the spell of the clouds of ever-changing colour that came up from below, of the depraved clang-tints of this perverted Dies Irae that sounded from an invisible source, and of an unfamiliar, pungent aroma.

Suddenly, a woman in a black cloak crept through the dancers to the centre of the floor. Simultaneously, the room became black with darkness and the music stopped. There was absolute silence.

When Byron could see again, he was aware that he and Lasca, together with all the others, were huddled against the vermilion velvet hangings. A pale, hideous, green glow suffused the room. The woman in the black cloak stood alone, perfectly motionless, in the centre of the glass floor. Now a pipe—oh, so far away—began to wail and there was a faint reverberation of the tom-tom. A cylinder of fierce white light shot up from below and enclosed the woman, playing in little ripples on the black satin of her cloak. A bell in the distance tinkled feebly and the cloak fell to the floor.

The girl—she could have been no more than sixteen—stood entirely nude. She was pure black, with savage African features, thick nose, thick lips, bushy hair which hovered about her face like a lanate halo, while her eyes rolled back so far that only the whites were visible. And now she began to perform her evil rites. . . . Byron groaned and hid his face in his hands. He could hear Lasca emitting little clucks of amazement. Standing before him, she protected him from the horror . . . while she watched. When he looked again, the light on the body was purple; the body was purple. The girl lifted a knife. . . . A woman shrieked. The knife . . .

Three days later, awakening at four in the afternoon, after his bath, Byron drew on a cerise burnous which Lasca had discovered for him in one of her chests of foreign treasures, and sought her, as usual, in the drawing-room. Although it was April, it was still slightly chilly, and he found her, in a clinging dressing-gown of sea-green, sitting before the fire, a half-filled glass of absinthe and water on a table beside her.

As he kissed her, she pushed him away, gently but impatiently.

Sit down, she said quietly. I want to talk to you.

He attempted to join her on the chaise-longue.

No, over there, she directed. I said I wanted to talk to you.

He obeyed her.

What have you been doing?

Loving you, my golden-brown, since the beginning of the world.

Yes, yes! I know all that, she retorted. I mean

what were you doing with yourself before you met me.

I wanted to be a writer.

A writer! What kind of writer?

He told her the story he had conceived.

Are you interested in the race? she demanded, scorn in her tone.

I'm interested in you.

That's no answer. Giving him no opportunity to reply, she rapidly went on, Yes, I suppose it might be said of me that I am a Negro, but as I once informed you, I never permit that fact to make any difference. I loathe the race. Niggers are treacherous and deceitful. You'll never get anywhere if you depend on them. Why, that silly Sylvia actually tried to take a man away from me one night. I had my revenge. I showed her up for the weak, pitiful thing she really is. Well, they detest me because I get what I want. They'll hate you if you're a good writer and yet in that foolish story of yours you make out an ironic defence for them.

It's only a story, after all, Byron commented lamely.

I know—only a story. Well, let me tell you something. . . . Her tone was bitter and hard. . . . If you want to write about Niggers, show them up. Hit them, bully them! These race-leaders! These uplifters! They all make me sick. The black motto is: Drag down the topmost, no matter how much his influence might help you to rise. Put the rollers under him! Get rid of him. He's a menace. . . . I know, she went on. I've been through it. Don't imagine I haven't had to struggle. Christ! . . . She bowed her head in her flattened palms. . . . I've been hounded—until, thank God, I became too strong for the pack. They can't crucify me again. When they try, I crucify them.

She began to sob passionately.

Lasca! Lasca darling, don't do that! He was by her side on the instant.

Wiping the tears from her eyes, she pushed him away.

These Niggers! she cried. Well, I learned about life from them. They taught me to kick my rivals. They taught me to hate everybody who got more than I did. And I'll say this: they gave me the strength with their dirty tricks to lift myself out of the muck and mire they call Negro society. There isn't one of 'em, at that, who would dare thwart me, cross my path. Let them dare. . . . Now she was raging . . . They know I'll beat them, beat them at their own game

Byron attempted to interrupt her. But . . . he began.

Let them alone! she screamed. They'll pull you down! They'll spit upon you! Always sweet to your face! Always charming—God, I'm sick of that Nigger charm—but behind your back a constant bickering and whispering. Gossip! Jealousy! Hatred! Smiles to your face, and a knife in the back.

Lasca!

Well, she continued, in a cold, calm tone, while I'm talking I might as well tell you that I don't think any more of you than I do of the others.

Lasca! He was on his knees before her. Don't say that! Don't say that!

I do say it. I'm using you just the way I use tooth-powder. After I'm done with your body I'll throw it out of the window, in the sewer, anywhere.

Lasca! Weeping softly, he buried his face in his hands. You can't mean that! I can't live without you!

You can't live without me! Hell, you can't. Forty men have said that and they're all walking the streets. White men and brown men, they're all the same. All. I use 'em until I tire of 'em and then I say, damn you and good-bye!

He raised his head to look at her. What he saw, the hideous distortion of the features, the tautness of the muscles of her throat, the glare in her eyes, terrified him.

You're just like all the others, you filthy Nigger kept boy.

Suddenly he flamed with rage. With a swift

movement he caught her throat in his strong hands and shook her violently.

You won't say that to me, you dirty bitch! he cried.

He flung her back on the chaise-longue and stepped away. Her hair dishevelled, she was gasping for breath, her tongue lolling out, but she lifted her arms feebly and beckoned him.

Kiss me, Byron, she panted. I love you. You're so strong! I'm your slave, your own Nigger! Beat me! I'm yours to do with what you please!

• what!?
she got turned on by his violent outburst towards her.

Seven

During the next two days and nights Byron spent his every waking and sleeping hour with Lasca. There were rages, succeeded by tumultuous passions; there were peaceful interludes; there were hours devoted to satisfying capricious desires, rhythmical amours to music, cruel and painful pastimes; there were the artificial paradises. Then, late one afternoon, Byron awakened to find himself alone.

At first he had no true realization of what had happened. He threw back the covers to be certain she was not concealed beneath them. Then he sat bolt upright and called her name. There was no reply. Leaping from the bed, he peered into the bathroom. No one there. Turning back, he sought a clue. The dress she had worn the previous evening lay crumpled on the floor where she had dropped it. Her chiffon undergarments, her stockings, her little silver shoes, were scattered about promiscuously. From the dresser, however, he missed her watch and her rings. He sensed a premonition of disaster. She was gone! Standing quite still in the centre of the floor, he tried to conceive what life would be without her.

He pushed the button in a panic of apprehension. Presently the maid appeared.

Where is Mrs. Sartoris? It was vain to attempt to control his voice: it vibrated with anxiety.

She's gone out.

When is she coming back?

She didn't say, the maid replied, and Byron was aware that she spoke with a new and not entirely respectful manner.

Will you have your coffee now? she inquired.

Please.

Byron closed the window, shutting out the chill air, but he left the curtains open. Bright, April sunshine flooded the room. In the bath he found the water too warm. Its tepidity irritated his nerves. Releasing the cold stream, he felt relieved as it stung his aching flesh. When, stepping out of the tub, he towelled himself, his body had become numb. No tingling, just a dead emptiness without sensation that extended to his very toes. While he was dressing an incident occurred which shattered him completely. For the first time in his life he drew the left shoe on the right foot. Aware of what this portent threatened, he tremblingly altered this condition.

He was adjusting his cravat when Marie appeared with the tray.

Just set it down, he said, adding, I'm going out. If Mrs. Sartoris returns, tell her that I'll be back soon.

Why had he announced that he was going out? Why had he dressed in such haste? He knew now. He could not rest a single instant in this apartment without her. It was necessary not only to his peace of mind, but to his very existence that he discover her at once. Leaving his breakfast untouched, he sought his hat and coat and rushed out, slamming the door behind him.

On the sidewalk he hesitated once more, doubtful which way to turn. How could he expect to find her? Where might she conceivably have gone? In the despair of indecision, he was aware of a touch on his arm. Turning, he looked into a smiling black countenance. The man, in chauffeur's uniform, lifted his cap and pointed across the street.

That's Mrs. Boniface's car, he announced. She told me to get you.

Did she . . . ? Byron began and then stopped, realizing that Adora would have explained nothing to this servant. He followed his guide silently and entered the car, his spirits soaring. It must be that Lasca had sent for him. How otherwise would Adora know his whereabouts? As they drove away, his heart was warm with hope.

Fairly leaping out of the car before Adora's house, he plunged down the steps and pressed the bell-button. A maid presently answered the summons.

I am Byron Kasson, he cried. Is . . . ?

Come right in, Mr. Kasson. Rest yo' coat.

She led him upstairs. The drawing-room was empty. Byron paced impatiently back and forth.

At last he saw Adora coming towards him down the stairs.

Where is Lasca? he demanded.

Adora was in the room now. Sit down, please, she invited him, adding, I haven't the slightest idea.

Byron ignored the invitation.

How did you find me then? he inquired.

All Harlem knows where you've been passing your time. I told my chauffeur to keep the car standing outside until you came out *alone*. It's not been very convenient for me to do without my automobile for two days.

Then why did you do it? To what special kind of interest am I indebted for this attention?

Oh, please sit down and stop shouting at me.

He obeyed her. After all, perhaps she knew something. Perhaps she could help him find *her*.

Adora, seated facing him, inquired, Has she left you?

Yes. No! What do you mean?

So you've lost her. Well, let me tell you something: you'll never see her again, at least not on the same terms.

You know . . . ! he shot out.

I know this much, she interrupted him, that when Lasca's through, she's through.

You're a liar!

Adora paused for a moment before she replied.

Obviously she was making a tremendous effort to control her temper. At last she continued, You're a very rude young man, as well as a very foolish one. If I hadn't asked you here for a particular reason, I don't think I'd . . .

She stopped and he, in his impotent rage, was silent.

I repeat, Adora went on firmly, when Lasca's through, she's through. I know her like a book, in and out. She's as hard as steel.

Don't you dare say a word against her!

I won't even mention her name again if you don't. After all, you spoke of her first. What I want to talk about is Mary.

So she's been blabbing!

See here, young man, if you jump at conclusions like that, it's no wonder you commit impulsive acts that no one in his right senses would be capable of. No, Mary hasn't been blabbing, but it's plain to be seen that she thinks of nothing but you. She loves you, that's the simple fact. You certainly don't deserve it. Nevertheless she loves you and nobody else.

She'll get over it, he countered bitterly.

Unfortunately for her, she will *not,* Adora retorted sternly. It's either you or nobody.

She puts on airs. She thinks she's too good for me. He was whining now.

You mean you think you're too good for her. Why, you're not worth her little finger-nail.

I know it, Byron admitted. I'm not. So don't you think it's just as well to let things stand as they are?

Personally, I certainly do think so, Adora averred. As a matter of fact, I advised her to marry Randolph Pettijohn.

The Bolito King!

Himself.

Why, you wouldn't want her to marry a man like that, would you?

Rather any *man* than a poor thing like you! Her voice was harsh. Rannie's self-made. He's a rough diamond. He isn't educated, but at least he's good and kind. He's a *man,* she affirmed. He would have made her a good husband. I told her so. She couldn't see it. She turned him down the day she met you.

The day . . .

Yes, at my house on Long Island, and I've always thought you were the reason she turned him down.

That isn't possible. I scarcely saw her that day.

I don't care. I believe it was the reason. Do you know anything about Mary? She's always been noted for her coldness towards men. Then you come along and she reacts like a volcano that has smouldered for years and unexpectedly begins to toss hot rocks into the air. . . . It doesn't seem to me that you are particularly unusual or desirable. Oh, you're good-looking enough, but just a light-weight, after all. Nevertheless, Mary wants you. She almost murdered Lasca at the Charity Ball. You must know that.]

I knew she was jealous.

She loves you, you ape. Anyway, she doesn't want to murder Lasca any longer. All she wants is to have you back. She can't work. She can't sleep. She can't even cry any more. Now, you just chase around and cheer her up.

No! Byron's face was hard.

What!

I won't.

You're not going back to that cheap brown-skin again, are you?

I'm going back to Lasca.

Well, she won't let you in.

I don't believe you.

She's through. Remember I know Lasca. I tell you she's through.

I'm going back, Byron shouted. Nobody can stop me.

For all I care you can go to hell, Adora cried. It would be better for Mary if you do.

I'm going back, he repeated doggedly.

Wait a minute. Olive was speaking. Byron, sitting with his back towards the doorway, had not observed her entrance.

I heard what you said just now, Byron, she went on, and I want to talk to you.

It's no good, Ollie.

No good! Olive's tone was scornful. I wonder, she went on, if you'll ever collect any brains. If it wasn't for Mary, I wouldn't mutter a single peep.

Tell her to forget me.

She can't. It's downright too bad, but she can't. Don't think you've fooled me. I can see the wall over there straight through you. You had to struggle a little in New York, but not very much at that. I know a hundred fellows who have had a harder time and have come through. I've watched you and I *know* you. You're lazy and soft and conceited. You're weak and touchy and proud and obstinate and bad-tempered. You won't have anything to do with really worth-while people like the Sumners and the Underwoods or the young literary group . . . or Howard . . . because they've got ahead in life while you're a failure. You even resent Mary because she loves you enough to want to help you and so she can't be bothered to lie to you and flatter you. Why, you poor thing you, if I were Mary I'd wait for a muddy day and use you as a doormat!

Like to hear yourself talk, don't you! he cried. Well, just listen to this: I'm going back to Lasca.

I know all about that, Olive replied wearily. I know how long that'll last. Well, she turned to Adora, I suppose we've done all we can. Let him return to his vomit. Her lip curled.

Yes, echoed Adora, let him go back. She lighted a cigarette.

Without a word more, Byron rushed downstairs, drew on his coat, and dashed out of the house.

So this had been a trap! Never in his life had he been so furious. His blood was seething. Damn meddling women! He ran all the way back to Lasca's apartment, a matter of four blocks.

He entered the hallway just too late to catch the ascending elevator. Too impatient to wait for its return, he bounded up the stairs, three at a time, until he stood facing Lasca's door on the fourth landing. Breathless, he pushed the button.

Marie opened the door cautiously.

Mrs. Sartoris has not come back, she announced and was about to close the door in his face when he prevented her by inserting his foot in the opening.

I want to come in and wait, he insisted.

My orders are to keep you out.

Why, my clothes are here!

Harry took your clothes back an hour ago.

My clothes . . . ! By God, I will come in! He forced himself past the maid.

Miss Lasca, screamed Marie, I'm being murdered!

The door leading to the drawing-room was flung violently open. Lasca stood framed in the opening.

How dare you break into my house! she cried. Get out of here!

Falling on his knees before her, he clasped her waist in his arms.

Lasca, he implored her, what have I done?

Her tone was ice. You haven't done anything. You bore me. Get out of here before I have you thrown out.

She struck him in the face. Rising unsteadily to his feet, he stepped backwards. Rage swelled the veins of his temples.

Damn you! he cried. Damn you!

Before he could make a single aggressive movement she had covered him with a revolver.

None of that, she said.

He hesitated.

So, she taunted him, you don't love me enough to want me to kill you! You're a coward as well as a bore, a filthy Nigger coward!

He slunk towards the outer door.

Get out! she went on. Get out and stay out! Marie, tell the boys downstairs never to allow this slimy garbage in the building again.

As the door slammed behind him, he almost collapsed. He was dazed. This was all so unexpected. Last night she had loved him as usual. Now . . . He did not know what had happened or why. He crept slowly down the stairs and out into the sunshine.

Through a blur he saw a limousine drawn up by the kerb before him. He vaguely recalled that it had been there when he entered the building. Approaching the car, he stooped to decipher the initials painted on the door. R. P., he read. R. P.?

He tried to think. There was something familiar about these letters. He turned to the chauffeur.

Whose car is this? he demanded.

The fellow regarded him with astonishment.

Why, doan you know dis heah cah? Ebberybody know dis cah. Dis cah, sir—the man drew himself up—dis cah heah et belong to Mr. Randolph Pettijohn.

Eight

From that instant Byron began to hate and to hate virulently. The world was coloured by his mood to an extent where he saw storms and muddy pavements despite the fact that the sun was shining. He had been made a fool of, that was his plaint, not alone by *her,* but by every one. All had conspired, it would appear, to make him out a complete ass. One of his first acts, induced by his blind, unreasoning fury, was to purchase a revolver.

A revulsion followed in which he sank into a state of utter depression. And now his guilty conscience reminded him of Mary, Mary who still loved him in spite of his treatment of her. Mary whose advice he had scorned. Perhaps she had been right to try to persuade him to see more influential people. If only he could have humbled his pride sufficiently to call on the Sumners, his affairs might have moved more prosperously. It was not alone the Sumners that he had neglected, to his own undoing, it was the social background they represented. He had missed all that and he had only himself to blame. His father had provided him with letters which would have opened all doors for him. His dear, old father who had forgiven him his misdeeds, who had even been patient during these last few awful months of futility and strife.

Byron began to comprehend vaguely how superficial his writing must have appeared. He had never suffered before, never really lived; certainly he had never had any self-understanding. Probably Durwood had been right. At any rate, he was now capable of the realization that Durwood had not intended to patronize him.

Well, it was too late. Too late to seek out the Sumners or their friends. Too late to ask Mary to forgive him. Whatever will become of me? he moaned.

This mood of self-reproach was not permanent. Fierce anger returned to control his spirit. How he loathed this woman who had made a fool of him! How he hated his successor in her affections! Governed by his rage, he clutched his revolver and cried aloud to the four walls of his room in which, like a dying animal, he had shut himself: I'll kill her! I'll kill him! I'll kill them both! But the revolver dropped from his relaxed fingers to the table, and his head followed. Weak, that's what he was, weak. God! he demanded imploringly, why haven't I the strength to go through with it?

Sensing his desperation, perhaps, Mrs. Fox was more than ordinarily kind. Discovering that he would not eat in the kitchen, she sought him out and tempted him with a tray of southern delicacies—she was a good cook. To please her, he tried to eat, and failing, recalled with shame how much he had disliked this good woman. *He* had been the snob, not these others. . . .

Late that afternoon he was lying in bed in his dark, little chamber, cursing his fate, groaning over the mess he had made of his life, hating Lasca more than ever, swearing to shoot Pettijohn, when there came a knock at his door. He did not immediately reply, but when the knock was repeated he called out, Who is it?

The door opened slowly to disclose Mrs. Fox silhouetted against the light in the hallway.

Dere's a lady heah to see you, honey, she announced.

A lady! He was on his feet at once. Show her in!

His heart was thumping furiously. Nevertheless, he summoned sufficient presence of mind to thrust his revolver under the pillow.

Another figure stood in the doorway.

Mary! he cried. Turning quickly to his table, he stroked the surface with his palm, searching a match. He lighted the gas-jet.

Now he faced her. How he longed to take her in his arms! Instead, his pride created a new belligerency.

Love was in his heart, but his lips formed these words: I suppose you came here to laugh at me.

She sank wearily on the bed. It was plain to be

seen that she had been weeping. As she sat there shrouded in her black cloak, she was wistful, appealing, but his nature refused his sympathy any open expression.

Byron, how can you be so cruel?

Then you've come here to pity me! Now he was sneering.

I've come because I love you. I couldn't help coming. Oh, she sobbed, can't you pity *me?*

I suppose Olive has told you I've been thrown over. I suppose you've come here to gloat.

She looked at him in bewilderment. Do you love her so much? she asked.

Love her! I hate her!

Then it is true: you do love her. She spoke with resignation.

How pathetic she was, how sweet. His only desire was to embrace her, to freely confess his folly, but his perverse pride strangled his desire.

Perhaps I do. What business is that of yours?

This speech actually hurt him more than anything that Lasca had said to him.

Forget about me, he cried passionately. You've come here to look me over. Well, enjoy yourself. I'm a failure, a failure in everything. Nobody has any use for me. Lasca has thrown me out. I'm living here like a swine. You ought to be happy!

Byron, how can you say these terrible things? You're not yourself. Don't you understand that I love you? she pleaded. I came here because I love you. I couldn't help coming, but if you don't love me at all, if you won't talk to me, what can I do?

He was silent.

Dear Byron, if you ever want me, if you ever need me . . . With a pitiful little cry, she rose and swiftly left the room.

A moment later he heard the closing of the outer door. Then and then only he cried out of the misery in his soul, Mary! Mary! There was no reply. Rushing to the hallway he flung open the outer door. She had disappeared. He did not follow her downstairs. Returning to his room, he knelt before his bed, burying his head in the covers.

Mary, he sobbed, dear little Mary, I do love you, but I can't go back to you until I've proved how much I hate *her*.

At this moment he made a swift decision and his hand crept slowly toward the object concealed beneath the pillow.

Nine

At midnight he entered the Black Venus. This resort was usually crowded at any hour between twelve and six in the morning. On this particular night there were so many people present that nearly all the space ordinarily reserved for dancing was occupied by tables. Byron, indeed, was forced to take a chair at a table at which four persons were already sitting. He ordered a quart of gin.

A girl with peppercorn hair, with a band of freckles across the bridge of her yellow nose, moved from table to table, singing through the din:

Baby, lovin' baby,
Won't you come home today?
Ah been cryin' an' a-cryin'
Ever since you went away.
Duh good Lawd knows
You hurt mah heart,
You took et lak a toy
An' you broke et all apart.
You kicked me roun' an slapped mah face,
But nobody else can take yo' place.
Ah'm gonna send a telegram
In a yaller envelope.
Gonna take a drink o' gin
To keep up hope.

Gonna git a sofa piller
An' kneel down an' pray,
Oh, baby, baby, baby,
Won't you come home today?

Byron subconsciously was aware of conversation at his table: Lawdy ain't her legs skinny! . . . She's no sheba. . . . Bank wouldn't pay today. Too many winners. Dey jes' wouldn't pay. . . . Was it duh nummer you was playin'? . . . Naw, Ah figgers Ah won 'cause Ah lost. . . . Sho' Ah knowed Siki. Useter strut down duh boulevards o' Paris wid a long, black coat, a stove-pipe hat, an' a glass in his eye, carryin' a monkey on his shoulder an' draggin' one yowlin' lion cub on a chain. He was nobody's business.

It all became a jumble in Byron's mind, a jumble of meaningless phrases accompanied by the hard, insistent, regular beating of the drum, the groaning of the saxophone, the shrill squealing of the clarinet, the laughter of the customers and occasionally the echo of the refrain,

Baby, won't you come home today?

A meaningless jumble. Like life. Like Negro life. Kicked down from above. Pulled down from below. No cheer but dance and drink and happy dust . . . and golden-browns. Wine, women, and song, and happy dust. Gin, shebas, Blues, and snow. However you looked at it. . . . Whatever you called it. . . .

He'd make it up with Mary after he got even with those two who'd made a fool out of him. He'd show 'em. Tomorrow he'd make it all right with Mary. Tomorrow he'd go to her and humble himself. How he hated Lasca! The whore! He'd show her!

Gert ain' here tonight . . . Won't you come home today? . . . Come along to duh washroom an' Ah'll give you a sniff . . . Snow am duh great pacifier. . . . Ah's goin' to play two hundred an' seben tomorrow. . . . Leanshanks Pescod's got a lef' . . . Harry Greb, Flowers . . . Gaze on dat hoofer . . . Ah done hates duh spring; Ah sighs fo' August ham. . . . Ax yo' mammy what makes she so black. . . . How come you do me lak you do, daddy?

He'd show 'em. He'd make 'em sorry. God, how he hated that she-devil. Byron drained another glass of straight gin.

The entertainer, having made the rounds of the tables, lifted her skirts to dance in a space on the floor near the band. Her pink, silk drawers, bordered with bands of lace with knots and bows of blue ribbon, were exposed.

Skinny legs! Too skinny! . . . Hey! Hey! . . . Doan care fo' dose high yallers. . . . Tum-tum! Tum-tum! Tum-tum!

Would that drummer never stop? Jungle! Savages! Amber moonlight! Why did that girl have a purple face? Rouge on chocolate. And that other girl was green as an olive. Powder on chocolate. Shebas, golden-brown shebas. Lousy Niggers, all of 'em. Drinking, laughing, sniffing snow, getting ready to push him down. . . . Pretty panties on that dancing sheba. To hell with her! To hell with 'em all!

He gulped down another glassful. Mary, sweet Mary, golden-brown *too*. She was his friend. She stuck by him. She wouldn't make a fool out of him. She . . . He'd get that black Nigger Pettijohn!

A couple at his table departed. The others still chattered: Been to Sam's new joint? . . . Pig's feet, hot-dogs, eggs. Pig's feet, hot-dogs, eggs. . . . A white-coated vendor stood over the table with a tray laden with food, each article wrapped in white tissue-paper. . . . Gimme . . . Ten cents . . . Dat's duh berries. . . . Gaze on dat gal wid duh monkey-chaser. . . . Dey's an achin' pain, dose monkey-chasers. We doan want 'em heah! Monkey land fo' duh monkey-chasers. . . . Look at Buddie wid Miss Annie. . . . Dat ain' Miss Annie, dat's kinkout. . . . Ah tells you et is Miss Annie, Buddie's gettin' keerless. Dose ofays stink powerful.

Doan never let yo' woman have her way;
Keep you in trouble all duh time,
Doan never let yo' woman have her way;
Keep you in trouble all yo' day.

Doan never have one woman fo' yo' frien';
When yo' out, nuther man in!

The music shivered and broke, cracked and smashed. Jungle land. Hottentots and Bantus swaying under the amber moon. Love, sex, passion . . . hate. Lef' side, right side! Git off dat dime. . . . The dancers swayed from one side to the other like sailors heaving an anchor. Black, green, blue, purple, brown, tan, yellow, white: coloured people!

In the tangle of dancers Byron caught a glimpse of Anatole Longfellow, dancing with . . . Where had he seen that girl? He knew he had seen her before. Yes, he remembered now: at the Winter Palace . . . with Randolph Pettijohn. Frightened eyes. He was her man; she was afraid. No woman afraid of me. Made a fool out of me. Hate her! Hate 'em all! . . . Doan never git one woman on yo' min' . . . Byron filled his glass.

The Creeper and his girl sat down in the two deserted places at Byron's table.

'Toly, you sho' is one bardacious scroncher.

You's goin' git scronched.

Ah'll tell duh world dat Ah can stir et roun',
Stir et roun'.
Takes a gal lak me to bake a cake up brown,
Cake up brown.

a new entertainer boasted through a megaphone.

Ah ain' had no hours ob happiness an' ease sence Ah lef' you, 'Toly.

Shet up!

Pacify yo'self, 'Toly. Pacify yo'self. Doan git recited.

The Creeper scowled.

Jungle, jumble. Waiters with shields, bearing poisoned wine: waiter-warriors. . . . Ah can stir et roun'. . . . Pink silk. Blue silk. That green girl. . . . What made her look green? Coloured girl, Byron remembered. That was it: coloured girl. If you've never been vamped by a brown skin. . . . Too skinny! Ain' she loose! Ah can stir et roun'.

Byron poured himself out another drink. What was going round and round in his head? My way, my way's cloudy; go send dem angels down! . . . Gin, golden-browns, Blues, and snow. Where did they get the snow? He wanted some. He was about to call a waiter when he heard a voice announce, Shine butter an' egg man. His weary eyes sought the doorway. Randolph Pettijohn! He thought he'd get him later with Lasca! Well, here would do. Res' yo' coat, he knew the girl was saying. The bastard! He'd soon rest his coat for ever! Byron's hand involuntarily sought his hip-pocket.

The King was walking towards him, straight towards him. The fool! All the waiters in the place surrounded him. *He* could have any table.

Nobody else good enough to keep a table if that black Nigger wanted it. He could hear them: Git up an' give Mr. Pettijohn yo' table. Any table for him. He'd show 'em! They'd never make a fool out of him again. How slowly the King was moving! He walked but he never seemed to come any closer.

Ah'll tell duh world dat Ah can stir et roun'. . . . Pzzz: a bullet whizzed past Byron's ear. A shriek . . . Pzzz! Another shot. Byron, dazed, turned his head. Weapon in hand, the Creeper stood poised for the fraction of a second. Yo' won't hitch on to no mo' mah gals! he muttered. Then like a streak he leaped through the crowd and disappeared through the doorway in the back wall. With a cry of 'Toly, the girl followed him. Pandemonium. Stampede. Glasses smashed. Tables upset. Shrieks. Cries. Howls. The room was empty.

Byron alone sat staring ahead of him. A fixed, blank stare. He was thinking how Paul Robeson looked when he sang Were you there? He remembered that he owed Howard a hundred dollars. Fingers like golden-brown chrysanthemum petals . . .

Then he saw the thing on the floor in a pool of blood under the amber moon. Fascinated, he crept slowly towards it.

Suddenly, he stamped on the face with the heel of his boot.

You Nigger bastard! he screamed.

He drew his revolver and shot once, twice into the ugly black mass.

Immediately his anger left him. The gun slipped from his fingers. His legs, shaking with terror, refused to support him. He sank to his knees.

Mary, he cried aloud, I didn't do it! I didn't do it!

He was curiously conscious that a white hand was reaching for the gun. He looked up to face a coat of blue buttoned with brass.

New York
March 1, 1926

Glossary of Negro Words and Phrases

arnchy: a person who puts on airs.
August ham: watermelon.
bardacious: marvellous.
berries, the: an expression of approbation.
blue: a very black Negro. Not to be confused with the Blues, Negro songs of disappointment in love.
Blue Vein Circle: after the Civil War the mulattoes organized themselves into a guild from which those who were black were excluded. This form of colour snobbery still persists in many localities.
Bolito: see Numbers.
boody: see hootchie-pap.
bottle it: equivalent to the colloquial English *shut up.*
buckra: a white person.
brick-presser: an idler; literally one who walks the pavement.
bulldiker: Lesbian.
charcoal: Negro.
C. P. T.: coloured people's time, *i. e.*, late.
Counsellor: a title often given to lawyers among coloured people.
creeper: a man who invades another's marital rights.
daddy: husband or lover.
dicty: swell, in the slang sense of the word.
dinge: Negro.
dogs: feet. Not to be confused with hot-dogs, frankfurters inserted with mustard between two halves of a roll.
Eastman: a man who lives on women.
fagingy-fagade: a white person. This word and the corresponding word for Negro are theatrical hog Latin.
happy dust: cocaine.
high yellow: mulatto or lighter.

hoof: to dance. A hoofer is a dancer, and hoofing is dancing.
hootchie-pap: see boody.
jig: Negro.
jig-chaser: a white person who seeks the company of Negroes.
kinkout: hair-straightener.
kopasetee: an approbatory epithet somewhat stronger than *all right*.
mama: mistress or wife.
Miss Annie: a white girl.
Mr. Eddie: a white man.
monk: see monkey-chaser.
monkey-chaser: a Negro from the British West Indies.
mustard-seed: see high yellow.
Numbers: a gambling game highly popular in contemporary Harlem. The winning numbers each day are derived from the New York Clearing House bank exchanges and balances as they are published in the newspapers, the seventh and eighth digits, reading from the right, of the exchanges, and the seventh of the balances. In Bolito one wagers on two figures only.
ofay: a white person.
papa: see daddy.
passing: i. e., passing for white.
pink: a white person.
pink-chaser: a Negro who seeks the company of whites.
punkin-seed: see high yellow.
scronch: a dance.
shine: Negro.
smoke: Negro.
snow: cocaine.
spagingy-spagade: Negro.
struggle-buggy: Ford.
unsheik; divorce.

The songs and snatches of Blues sung by characters on pages 34, 35, 52, 137, 139, 142, 144, 145, 146, 207, 246, 247, 248, 249, 277, 278 and 281 were written especially for *Nigger Heaven* by Mr. Langston Hughes.

A NOTE ON THE TYPE IN WHICH THIS BOOK IS SET

The type in which this book has been set (on the Linotype) is based on the design of Caslon. It is generally conceded that William Caslon (1692–1766) brought the old-style letter to its highest perfection and while certain modifications have been introduced to meet changing printing conditions, the basic design of the Caslon letters has never been improved. The type selected for this book is a modern adaptation rather than an exact copy of the original Caslon. The principal difference to be noted is a slight shortening of the ascending and descending letters to accommodate a larger face on a given body-size.

University of Illinois Press
1325 South Oak Street
Champaign, IL 61820-6903

www.press.uillinois.edu